Almut Grüntuch-Ernst
IDAS Institute for Design and
Architectural Strategies (Eds.)

HORTITECTURE

THE POWER OF ARCHITECTURE AND PLANTS

jovis

CONTENT

HORTITECTURE

MORE NATURE WITHIN THE ARTIFACT

HORTITECTURE is a term I have chosen to describe the search for synergies in the combination of architecture and plant material that could effectively enhance well-being and reduce our footprint on the built environment. The word is derived from the Latin *hortus*, or "garden," mixed with the word *architecture*. It is the search for the potential of plants as an integral part of architecture; not as a mimicry of nature, nor through engineering synthetic substitutes, but through the integration of living plant material.

HORTITECTURE aims beyond naive sentimentality and romantic glamorization. Not simply "back to nature," but a future-orientated, architectural way of thinking—taking plants off the ground into a new conceptual and spatial context.

1

2

3

4

5

6

1 Hanging Gardens of Babylon **2** Jean Baptiste Rondelet, 1833 **3** Temple of Angkor Wat, Cambodia **4** Green Roof Houses, Iceland **5** Malator House, Wales by Future Systems, 1998 **6** Not Red But Green, 2014 by Per Kristian Nygård

Plant material is the basis of building history and holds archaic, sensual power. Unlike solid building materials, which are fixed and controlled by the architect, living green materials challenge the design with dynamics of growth.

Some stigmatizing prejudices are connected to green architecture. The first one is "Verkrautung": a common term used in German when undesirable plants and weeds grow uncontrollably, hiding a lack of design quality by simply covering the building with a green hood. However, plants can be more than just a defensive device to erase the visual impact of architecture with a green shield that grows after the architect has left the project.

Very often green elements in buildings are reduced to a fashionable iconic addition with a distinct semiotic impact, building up a green label to sell the property investment on the market. "Greenwashing" or "green labeling" attempts to upgrade a weak project. A lack of conceptual, aesthetic, or ethical quality is disguised with a green cover that makes it look sustainable.

Large areas of the natural surface on this planet are covered with anthropocene structures. Humans are rapidly urbanizing natural environments—not only covering or sealing the surface with infrastructure and buildings, but also demineralising and exploiting the soil by turning fruitful cultivation into industrialized agriculture. Frei Otto called it the "sterilization" of the planet.

The coexistence of human beings and nature is out of balance and we are facing the backlash of thoughtless consumption. We need to address the philosophical question of how to approach ecosystems with a humble respect for life on this planet—human life and beyond. Healthy human life depends on diverse and resilient ecosystems.

1

2

3

4

5

6

1 Tree Hotel, Harads, Sweden by Tham & Videgard, 2009 **2** Casa de Vidro, Sao Paulo by Lina Bo Bardi, 1950 **3** Nordic Pavillion, Bienale di Venezia by Sverre Fehn, 1958–62 **4** Highrise of Homes by J. Wines, 1981 **5** Celestial Real Estate by J. Walker, 1909 **6** Bosco Verticale, Milan by S.Boeri, 2012

HORTITECTURE calls for architectural strategies that activate the potential of plant material in the design process—as part of the conceptual approach and the architectural articulation. It aims to understand and activate the potential of plant material for providing ecosystem services and improving the microclimatic conditions for healthy and liveable cities.

HORTITECTURE started off as a very open term to collect, classify, and study a wide spectrum of combinations of nature and artefacts. Projects that are made with, made for, or made from vegetative material are collected, building an archive of references. In order to compare the impact on the environment and the architectural design, we categorize the projects based on criteria linked to various benefits, maintenance, and resilience indicators.

Plants can be more than a decorative addition to the building. They can be an integral part of the building's ecological performance. Plants can produce food, absorb noise, pollution, carbon dioxide, and particulate matter, and plants can cool urban temperatures by transpiring water.

There are various architectural strategies for activating the building envelope with living vegetation: stacking gardens in layers will multiply green surfaces and their benefits. Overhangs and protrusions can also form a buffer around building objects and enclosed spaces.

Bosco Verticale (PAGES 20–29) is a milestone project that illustrates these principles and has received international recognition as a prototype building for the cities of tomorrow. The living green skin wraps around the residential tower adding a new quality of life to high-density housing, as well as improving the microclimatic conditions in the inner city of Milan. The elevated gardens have an impact on the urban scale: green façades absorb dust and CO^2, produce oxygen, and provide protection against sun and noise.

1

2

3

4

5

6

1 'Ring Around Tree' kindergarten, Tokyo, Japan by Tezuka Architects, 2007 **2** Green Cast, Japan by Kengo Kuma, 2011 **3** St Telmo Museum, San Sebastián by Nieto Sobejano, 2011 **4** Firma Casa, Sao Paolo by SuperLimão Studio + Campanas Brothers, 2011 **5** 'Hanging Gardens', Fünf Höfe, Munich by Tita Giese with Herzog & De Meuron, 1999–2003 **6** *Sticks and Stones*, Berlin by David Chipperfield, 2014

Architecture with plant material tries to balance the human condition with the built and natural environment. The visual and physical connection with the elevated garden changes the atmosphere within each apartment in the building. On the balcony of the high-rise you experience two different scales: you are sitting under a sheltering tree, and at the same time you are exposed to the view down onto the city of Milan. But you also experience a building as a habitat for humans that allows for the co-habitation of plants and animals.

In a time of increasing digitalization and dematerialization, close contact to plants in an urban/virtual environment provides a full sensual experience of nurturing life and passing time. It seems to be within human nature that we long to be close to trees—to build a human nest within the tree-tops, or wrap around their trunks as they grow within man-made artefacts. The installation *Sticks and Stones* by David Chipperfield at the Nationalgalerie in Berlin, is an homage to Mies van der Rohe, but also expresses a deep longing to reconcile and rebalance nature and the architectural artefact.

Poetic power can be derived from the combination of architecture and living plants. Compositions of grey and green layers negotiate the dynamic and magic balance of the elements. But it is not easy to handle living material in architecture. Living green material is dynamic—it challenges the design with the intrinsic characteristics of growth. How can architects generate and maintain a composition with living material?

The second field of research is architecture built from plant material. The building industry produces far too much waste and pollution, and we do not know how hazardous waste will ever be removed from this planet. In the search for more sustainable materials, architects can learn from vernacular wisdom by exploring the challenges and potentials of building with organic plant material.

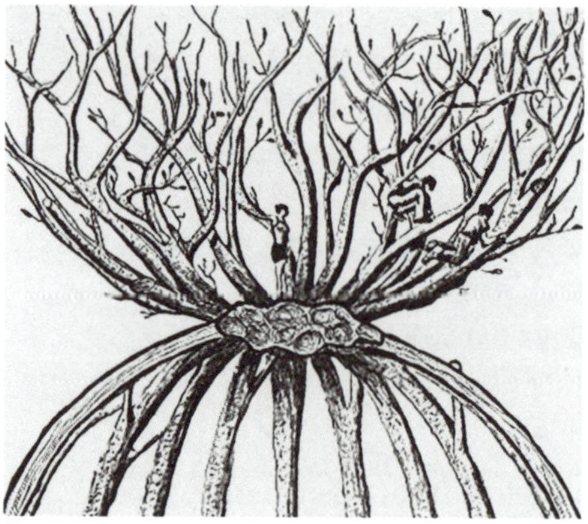

1

2

3

4

5

6

7

1 The Patient Gardener by Visiondivision, Anders Berensson & Ulf Mejergren, 2011 **2** Bamboo Pavillion by XuTianTian Architects, 2016 **3** Brooklyn Grange Rooftop Farm, 2010 **4** Public Farm 1 by WORK Archi Company, 2008 **5** Green House **6** Vertical Farm **7** Cilindrical Hydroponic Design by Omega Garden

Architects can learn a lot about sustainable construction from organic plant material by researching its vernacular application historically and across the world. When I first started as a student of architecture, I spent my summers working on traditional thatched roofs made of water reeds. I learned how the top of the roof is finished with living plants that grow their roots to physically connect the straw tops, while allowing for the airflow within. I see a great potential in the reinterpretation of this building tradition. The tactile quality and seamless elegance of this material are outstanding, and hold great potential for an aesthetic quality far beyond its stereotype. As far as sustainability is concerned, plants are a true cradle-to-cradle material, one that even acts as a thermal buffer with a high level of resilience.

In the past years the spectrum of timber construction has expanded enormously. Today, prefabrication and digitalization allow for more than standard timber beams and poles. Some architects use living plants as a construction material and go as far as growing buildings from plants; Baubotanik from Stuttgart, for example. They are studying how to construct multi-story buildings from growing trees.

The third field of research is architecture designed for plants in agricultural production. The industrialization of agriculture has reached its limits. For example, the production of pharmaceutical plants has become a real challenge, as there are hardly any places left on this planet without traces of contaminated water, soil, and air. To guarantee the purity of herbal products, plants are no longer exposed to a natural environment. To guarantee purity they are sealed off in closed systems—in buildings isolated from the natural environment. Man-made environmental catastrophes might make this research even more important in the future.

Urban farming has become a big trend: growing food in the city on rooftop gardens, close to the consumer, with educational and social benefits. For mass production, a new typology of industrial buildings will be developed for dense cities—greenhouse buildings sealed off in closed-circle systems.

HORTITECTURE SYMPOSIA

The first symposium was part of a research seminar to compare and analyse architectural solutions based on traditional and vernacular wisdom as well as recent explorations, and how these are fuelling the discourse in the field of architecture. During a series of public lecture days we invited speakers to present interdisciplinary projects and discuss discoveries and innovations, asking:

QUESTIONS

How are plants integrated within the building system? What kinds of benefits can a new kind of nature-artifact combination offer? How do the plantings affect the overall environment and architectural design? What is the aesthetic value and how can the composition be designed and maintained? What is the feedback—assumptions, expectations, failures, and surprises? What is the maintenance factor and how scalable are these new solutions?

In the symposia thereafter we maintained our commitment to these questions and widened our multi-layered approach towards knowledge exchange between disciplines. We invited experts from inside and outside the architectural discourse to gain a deeper understanding of the physical and biological properties of plants in architecture. In this publication, we present the speakers in the chronological order of the events. In the following paragraphs, we will outline their various relationships to themes such as ecosystem service provision, construction, urban food production, and the poetic power of built compositions.

ECOSYSTEM SERVICES

Architecture is part of an urban ecosystem. As such, it is affected by its environmental context and affects it. These mutual interactions should be taken into account in the design process. TU Braunschweig researchers Boris Schröder-Esselbach and Stefan Weber from the Institute of Geoecology directed our attention towards the patterns, processes, and functions of urban ecosystems and habitats. They defined and explained the concepts of ecosystem services and their relationship to human well-being and urban biodiversity, as well as the urban heat island and the manifold effects of green roofs (PAGES 58–63).

WATER MANAGEMENT

We also learned from the experts Marco Schmidt and Daniel Roehr who are researching and monitoring projects on urban ecology through the integration of green roofs, green façades, rainwater harvesting, and stormwater management (PAGES 110–113 & 184–193).

MICROCLIMA For the Austrian pavilion at the expo in Milan Klaus K. Loenhart created a forest inside a building (PAGES 132–139). In the city, we breathe in far too many polluted particles, so by entering the pavilion you experienced the micro-climatic conditions of a forest and you immediately understood that plants have healing powers in dense cities.

EUROPEAN CITY Milan, as a Smart City of the Future, hosted the 2015 expo focussing on our relationship with nature and food production. It is the first European city with a green high-rise, namely the experimental milestone building Bosco Verticale by Stefano Boeri (PAGES 20–33). He also developed a wider vision for Milan of how the derelict railway land could be transformed into green parks and connected into a "green river" with very few, very dense buildings at the perimeter (PAGES 120–123). Marion Waller worked as an advisor to the Deputy Mayor of Paris on the recent reinventer.paris competition. In the competition brief they asked explicitly for buildings that "increase biodiversity and create new habitats for flora and fauna" (PAGES 124–131). Jacob van Rijs of MVRDV explained how their office has experienced the "power of the green," starting with the expo pavilion in Hannover in 2000. Now they are responsible for the master plan of Floriade 2022—a model for the green city of the future (PAGES 42–51).

ASIAN HIGH DENSITY The green city politics of Milan and Paris represent the European city and climate. But we also focus on Singapore; a model city for hyper-dense, fast-growing Asian cities. WoHA Architects are consultants to the Urban Redevelopment Authority of Singapore, developing their vision of a "City in a Garden." They have built many super-dense high-rise buildings with generous green circulation spaces that connect communal gardens as informal meeting spaces for the inhabitants (PAGES 152–163). Christoph Ingenhoven explained his "super green" strategy for the Marina One project; a high-rise cluster for more than 20,000 people connected by vertical parks (PAGES 140–151). Many of these ideas connect back to the work of Ken Yeang, an architect and ecologist from Kuala Lumpur. He presented thirty years of work developing a new green architecture by connecting green spaces into a vertical linear park that wraps around high-rise buildings (PAGES 96–103). Vo Trong Nghia on the other hand, started at a small scale, bringing green into the hyperdense Asian city and designing his buildings to be shared by trees and humans.

CONNECTING WITH NATURE

Moreover, Vo Trong Nghia heightens children's awareness of nature in the kindergarten he designed where they learn to farm and harvest food on the rooftop (PAGES 72-83). Dan Wood, partner of WorkAC presented their PS1 installation and the "edible kindergarten," addressing the relationship between the urban, the rural, and the wild in New York City (PAGES 84-91). Maria Auböck told us about her experiences as a landscape designer trying to help nature thrive in the city and connect city-people to gardening on the roofs of their houses in Munich (PAGES 206-215).

PSYCHOLOGY

The environmental psychologist Nicola Moczek talked about the impact of vegetation on human beings in regard to their living and working environments (PAGES 92-95). Plants can provide social and emotional benefits. They help to balance the human condition in the city as a strategy to detox and destress from the built environment.

DESIGN CHALLENGE

However, living green material is a challenge to the architectural design. Although it is very easy for architects to produce a green rendering and illustrate a green vision, it is not so easy to predict the performance of the combination of plant life and built structures.

MAINTAIN AND REPAIR

Gerhard Zemp is a horticultural specialist consulting on new projects and improving existing projects like the Commerzbank tower by Sir Norman Foster in Frankfurt (PAGES 166-175). Architects have to team up with experts in biology and ecology to design and maintain such compositions.

COMPOSITIONS

International architects at the symposium presented how they have integrated buildings and plantings as architectural compositions. Fuensanta Nieto presented the façade of the museum in San Sebastian with an infiltration of grey and green layers that negotiate the dynamic balance of nature and artifact with poetic power (PAGES 34-41). Thomas Corbasson showed projects with compositions dissolving the boundaries of nature and buildings (PAGES 228-239). Elisabeth Kather, the project architect of many green projects at the office of Jean Nouvel, reported on milestone buildings in Cyprus and Sydney (PAGES 256-263).

Plants can do more than decorate surfaces and hide the architectural object. Plants can define spaces and become structural elements of a building. Living plant material is a dynamic material.

PLANT LIFE The biologist Dieter Volkmann told us about the stressful life of plants. His research is focused on communication in plants and the neuronal aspects of plant life (PAGES 216–221) which helps architects to understand the biological properties and behaviour of plants: materials full of life that grow in relation to light and gravity. At the University of Hohenheim, Alina Schick researched façade greening and the response to environmental stimuli like gravity, and later developed a system that allows plants to grow horizontally (PAGES 106–109).

GROWING CONSTRUCTIONS Ferdinand Ludwig and Daniel Schönle, the pioneering architects in the field of living plant constructions presented fascinating experiments with plants joined to construct multistory buildings—buildings that literally continue to grow (PAGES 64–71). Wilfrid Middleton is now also involved in this research and studies vernacular green constructions; he reported on living bridges in India (PAGES 176–183). The artist Diana Scherer experiments with the poetic growth of plant material. Her art is made by growing plant roots into inspiring textiles (PAGES 248–255).

FOOD PRODUCTION Susanne Thomaier presented research at the TU Berlin on urban farming in and on buildings, summarized as Zero-Acreage Farming (PAGES 222–227). An ecologist at the German Aerospace Center, Gerhild Bornemann, reported on the development of closed biological systems for space applications and their terrestrial applicability in future agricultural systems, including urban farming (PAGES 114–119). Tomás Saraceno shared his future scenario of flying gardens: food production in airborne structures high above the city (PAGES 52–57). Niklas Weisel developed new technologies for textile-based vertical greening and farming. He also develops leasing concepts for urban farmers activating vertical surfaces in cities (PAGES 240–247). Chris Precht presented projects by Penda Architects. They have developed a vision for dense housing structures based on green modular systems that integrate multiple private gardens for local food production very close to consumers (PAGES 194–205).

The goal of this book is to provide an accessible overview to the field of HORTITECTURE, documenting the multidisciplinary research presented at the symposia. Thirty-three experts share ideas while building up awareness, critical reflection, and competence for a more nature-based architecture.

Symposium 2014

Stefano Boeri
Fuensanta Nieto
Jakob van Rijs
Tomás Saraceno
Boris Schröder-Esselbach
Stefan Weber
Ferdinand Ludwig
Daniel Schönle
Vo Trong Nghia
Dan Wood
Nicola Moczek
Ken Yeang

VERTICAL FOREST

With the Bosco Verticale or the Vertical Forest—an exceptionally greened residental highrise in Milan, STEFANO BOERI and his studio gained worldwide attention and created a manifesto to stop the mineralization of urban surfaces, by rebalancing urban, agricultural and natural spheres.

In his role as chief editor of the architectural journal *Abitare*, Boeri presented an installation for the Venice Architecture Biennale in 2009. Guided by the feeling that the term "sustainability" risked becoming rhetoric and obscuring the view of the real state of things, three dystopias of sustainability were sketched under the title "Paradoxes of Sustainability." Reflections on how to avoid these three dystopias and reconcile a balance between the urban sphere, the agricultural sphere and the natural sphere resulted in research with six directives on the possible evolution of Milan. One of these directives dealt with the Expo 2015 in Milan, which focused on the diet of the world's population.

STEFANO BOERI: "So we know quite well how much this topic is crucial for the future of the planet, and how much the question of food production is dependent on and aided by the relation and balance between agriculture, nature, and urban spheres. That's the idea behind of the first of the concept plans developed together with Jacques Herzog and Ricky Burdette, with the contribution of William MacDonough and with the very important contribution of Carlo Petrini, who is the president of Slow Food Association and International Association. The basic starting point of our proposal was to imagine the Expo site as a sort of huge planetary garden, where all the countries were invited to show how they can transform their agricultural products into food. The richest countries would display their advanced technology and the poorer countries their biodiversity. And so the idea was really to imagine a very simple grid with a space for every country to show its contribution to the issue of hunger. In a certain way this kind of concept was accepted at the beginning and then completely abandoned by the political leaders of Milan. The Expo will open in Milano next month. The Expo that took place in Milan in 2015 was a very important appointment for many reasons but it was quite different from its original concept: a sort of huge botanical garden, transforming the theme of the Expo itself into a space."

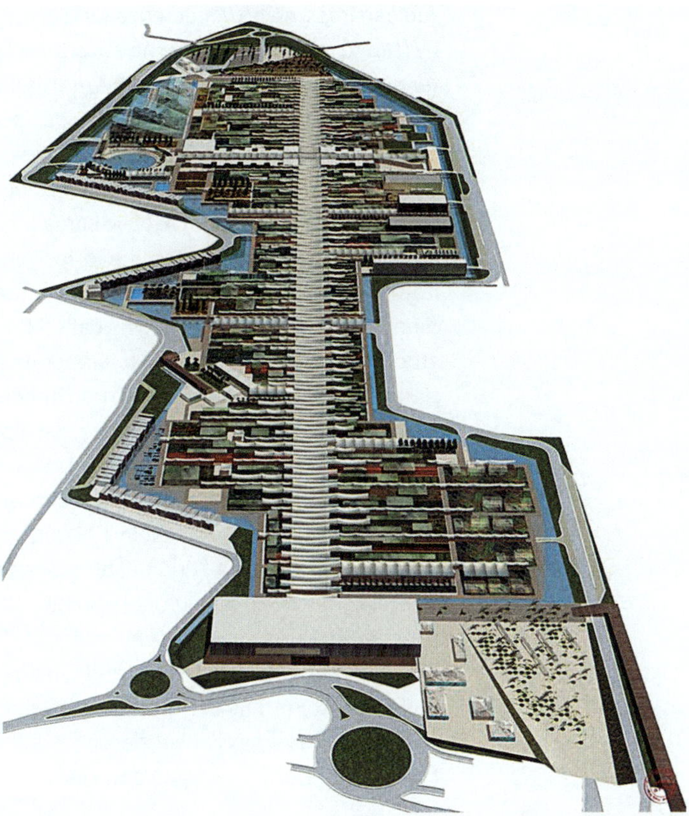

Masterplan
EXPO 2015

"It is essential to create a better natural environment while building, and we have to stop the mineralization of urban surfaces. We need to multiply the vegetable and the organic surfaces, horizontally and vertically—knowing that in the future we will be obliged to build high-rises not only out of necessity, to stop the consumption of natural and agricultural soil, but also because of the cost." STEFANO BOERI

"You can imagine how much this kind of effort was inspired by thinkers and artists of the seventies. With his tree tenant demonstration at the Milan Triennale in 1973, Friedensreich Hundertwasser was declaring that architecture must leave more space to nature. Fifteen tree tenants were planted in the façades along one of the main roads in Milan. For sure, we have some amazing experience and references from history, like Torre Guinigi in Lucca. In Italy in the seventies we had, thanks to the radical movement, a group of architects who called themselves Superstudio and were really trying to elaborate a new kind of parallel between natural and urban spheres. Probably one of the most sophisticated projects, developed by Andrea Branzi with Domus Academy, is Agronica, an agricultural environment also hosting an urban settlement. Joseph Beuys at Documenta Kassel in 1982 came with this amazing idea to transform 7000 basalt stones into 7000 oak trees, which have been brought and planted and irreversibly changed the Kassel urban environment. That's probably the most powerful, strongest, and most sensitive example of the way to rethink the relationship between city and nature; in the version of a different relationship between the mineral word and organic world."

"Looking for the advantages in the relationship between architecture and nature lets us look at manifestos that describe the relationship between nature and the built environment with art: Hundertwasser, Superstudio, Villa Bransi, Beuys-Kassel 7000 Oaks 1982 ... as well as the manifesto Expo Milano and the Vertical Forest." STEFANO BOERI

1

2

3

4

5

Learning from Vertical Forest 01: 10 reasons
Imparare dal Bosco Verticale 01: 10 ragioni

1 **VF01 is a project for the environmental survivor of contemporary cities.**
BV01 è un progetto di sopravvivenza ambientale per la città contemporanea.

2 **VF01 multiplies the number of trees and plants in cities.**
BV01 moltiplica il numero di alberi e piante nelle città.

3 **VF01 is a tower for trees inhabited by humans.**
BV01 è una torre per alberi abitata da umani.

4 **VF01 is an anti-spawl device.**
BV01 è un dispositivo anti-sprawl.

5 **VF01 demineralizes urban surfaces.**
BV01 demineralizza le superfici urbane.

6 **VF01 reduces the pollution of the urban environment.**
BV01 riduce l'inquinamento nell'ambiente urbano.

7 **VF01 reduces energy consumption.**
BV01 riduce i consumi energetici.

8 **VF01 is a multiplier of urban biodiversity.**
BV01 è un moltiplicatore della biodiversità.

9 **VF01 is an ever changing urban landmark.**
BV01 è un landmark cangiante.

10 **VF01 is a living ecosystem.**
BV01 è un ecosistema vivente.

1 Friedensreich Hundertwasser on the occasion of the Milan Triennale, 1973 **2** Torre di Guinigi di Lucca **3** Superstudio, *The Continuous Monument* **4** Andrea Brnazi with Domus Academy, Agronica **5** Joseph Beuys at Documenta Kassel in 1982

BOSCO VERTICALE
MILAN, 2014

Through the opportunity to realize two high-rise buildings in the center of Milan, Boeri Studio started to think about how to plant a forest of two hectares in an urban surface of 2000 square meters, and how leaves can contribute to the reduction of pollution, absorb CO^2, produce oxygen, absorb the dust produced by urban traffic, and so on. They formed an interdisciplinary group with engineers and botanists.

"One of the main issues regards irrigation, that is able to support such an amount of plants. The integrated water cycle collects the rainwater, reuses the grey water from the apartments, and is basically powered by a geotechnical pump, using the groundwater which is in the soil of Milan with the idea of storing the water after its use for irrigation. We selected the trees from 3 to 9 meters high, one by one in relation to the kind of humidity you have at different heights and with the sun exposure. Also, we were absolutely aware of the necessity to select trees capable, for instance, of demonstrating the capacity to filter the sunlight in the summertime. At the same time, on the northern façade of the two towers, it is evident that it is better to have trees that lose their leaves in the winter in order to let the sunlight enter the apartment."

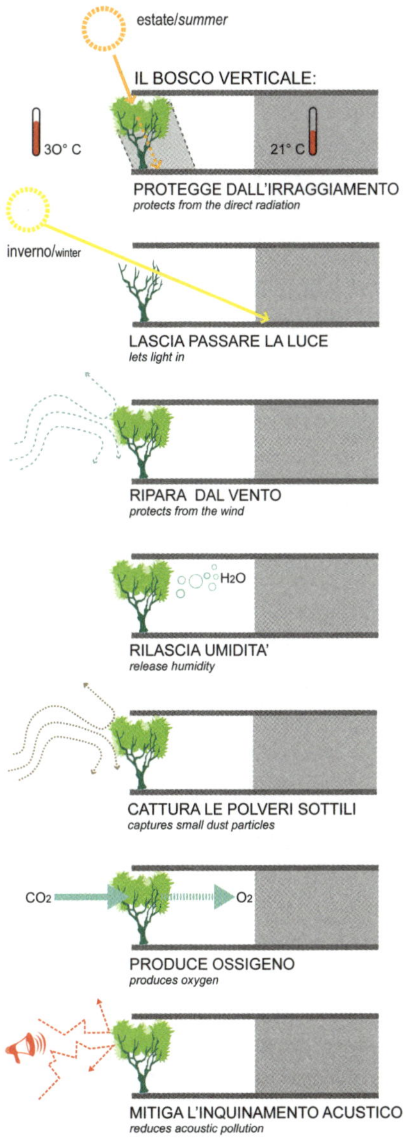
estate/summer
IL BOSCO VERTICALE:
3O° C
21° C
PROTEGGE DALL'IRRAGGIAMENTO
protects from the direct radiation
inverno/winter
LASCIA PASSARE LA LUCE
lets light in
RIPARA DAL VENTO
protects from the wind
H2O
RILASCIA UMIDITA'
release humidity
CATTURA LE POLVERI SOTTILI
captures small dust particles
CO2
O2
PRODUCE OSSIGENO
produces oxygen
MITIGA L'INQUINAMENTO ACUSTICO
reduces acoustic pollution

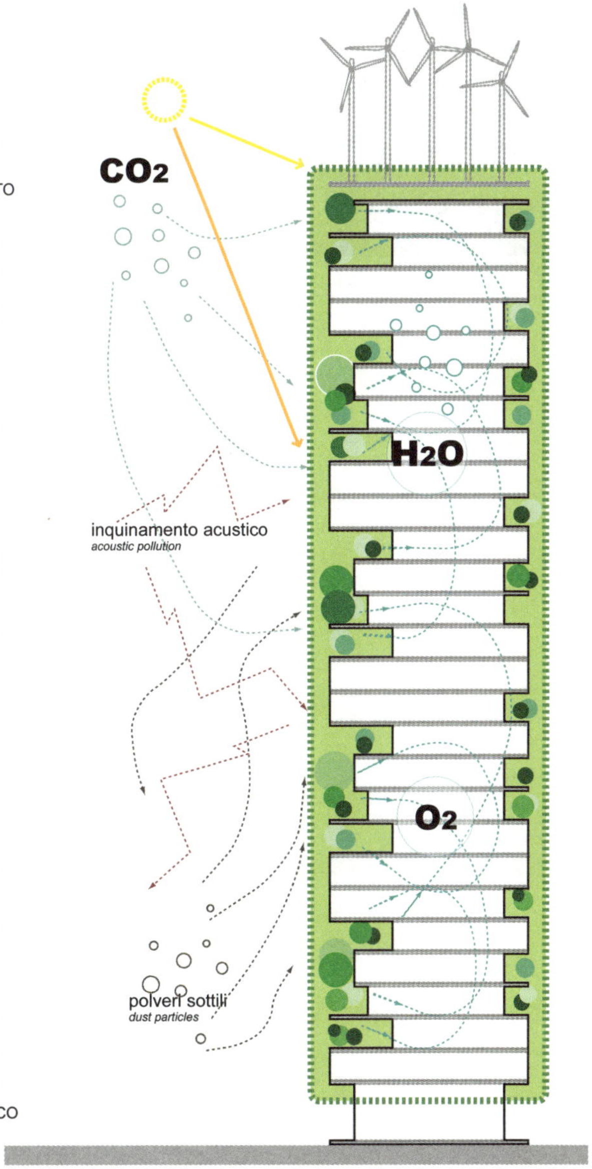
CO2
H2O
inquinamento acustico
acoustic pollution
O2
polveri sottili
dust particles

"To have a tree at a height of 110 meters means dealing with possibly extremely windy conditions. Through special wind tunnel tests at the University of Florida, we found out that the bigger the trees are, the more resilient they are, and the better their resistance to the wind is. This is one of the things I have learned from working together with specialists like the botanists and structural engineers that observe the behavior of the trees. Those tests assured us that we can put bigger trees up higher. The composition of the soil was also very important. The soil has to not be too heavy, for sure, in containers 1 meter by 1.20 meters, but at the same time, the soil has to be heavy enough to hold, to bring, to conserve, and to ensure the roots don't move in windy conditions.

Another big point is the management: the maintenance of more than 21,000 plants. We have around 800 trees, 4,500 shrubs and 15,000 smaller plants. The idea was to imagine first that the entire 'green' part is a sort of common good, shared by the owners of the apartments. That was, in a certain sense, a necessary step in order to see how else it would be possible to maintain the building. The green part of the balconies is considered collective property, so the maintainence is centralized.

I think what is really relevant is the relation to biodiversity and to the possibility of having a significant number of living organisms in the center of a highly polluted and hyper—dense urban environment. So that's, I think, the most challenging point of the Bosco Verticale project—and we know very well that biodiversity is not just about green. We should also take into account the fact that we are producing, introducing a population of insects that are fighting against the parasites. The trees are grown without the use of pesticides and so there is a much more heterogeneous population of birds that are now starting to inhabit the two towers than are typically present in Milan.

The project has been followed by the BBC team that has installed three main cameras all around in order to study not the residents, but—for example—habitats, growth, and biodiversity, like the birds and how they move and define their ecosystem. We are engaged in continuous dialogue with several universities. We are a case study."

“The project introduces as much nature to the urban environment as possible. The idea is that for every human, there should be place to sustain four birds and butterflies, two trees, eight shrubs and twenty-two plants. It is a contribution to biodiversity ... the project is an experiment that should be followed and monitored. We need to see how the seasonal changes work and become a part of the changing façade.”

STEFANO BOERI

"I think this is an experiment. Let me be very honest—it's nothing more than an experiment. It is an ongoing process which has to be followed because if we are in a way quite sure about the reaction of the trees, the proportion as you have seen is one human to two trees, eight shrubs and twenty other plants. We really tried to do our best to predict every possible consequence related to the life of the trees. The proximity, in terms of three-dimensional relations between the balconies and the leaves of your neighbors is such that they sometimes come down from the floor, invading the windows of your room. So all this has to be monitored, and that's the reason we are following this kind of reaction. At the same time, it is extremely important to imagine what will happen when the leaves or the groundcover plants fall down from the balcony. We have worked a lot in order to solve troubles and issues that have never been faced by the architectural discipline, and so we were in a way obliged to spend a lot of time and involve a lot of different experts in order to overcome some of these troubles.

Jilles Clement, a French landscape designer and important thinker on this topic, came to visit the Bosco Verticale. He told me that what he likes about the project is that it is not spectacular. Indeed, there is nothing spectacular about the aesthetic of the building. It is a very sober building. So what Jilles liked about the building was nature being the protagonist. Sometimes architecture can contribute to modernization and innovation and transformation, and should take this kind of second-line approach to the transformation. I feel that architecture should serve as a pedestal for nature rather than as a self-celebrating entity. That is an important contribution. It is essential to create a better natural environment while building."

"Today there is an overwhelming extension of the urban sphere that has nothing to do with the traditional European urban pattern. This condition is transfiguring the landscape. We need to repair this by re-differentiating between three spheres—creating a transition state between city, nature, and agriculture. By extending the specific bio-dimension, we can create a much more specific architecture. Urban towers will look different in different climates." STEFANO BOERI

POETIC COMBINATION

FUENSANTA NIETO, co-founder of the architecture practice NIETO SOBEJANO ARQUITECTOS based in Madrid and Berlin, sees their work as essentially context-based, which in some cases requires a fusion with nature. This relationship between the plant and the building is aimed at all senses and often unfolds a unique poetic quality.

SAN TELMO MUSEUM
SAN SEBASTIÁN, 2011

FUENSANTA NIETO: "When we entered the competition in 2011, we were asked to make an extension to the museum building. So what we decided to do was to refurbish the building and to work in that specific space—that space which was between the natural area of the city and the urban area of the city—and that way we were going to redefine this limit between natural and urban. We decided to build two walls, two inhabited walls, that through their geometry and interior spaces, were going to relate both to the already-existing areas of the mountain, which is called Mount Urgull, and also to the interior spaces of the already-built building. We touched the old building only at three points—in order to make the circulation work but not to aggravate the old architecture. The new San Telmo Museum is an addition to the old building, redefining the border between the natural and the urban within this very specific context. The wind and the sea had eroded the stone, and at the same time plants were coming out of the mountain. So we were trying to translate this situation into our project, into our façade."

"When we design with plants, we consider that they are going to change and try to foresee what might happen with the change. So it is not something that we can just let happen: you have to think in advance about how you want to control it. We must have a concept that works together with plants, but the architectural solution underneath must be determined and strong."

FUENSANTA NIETO

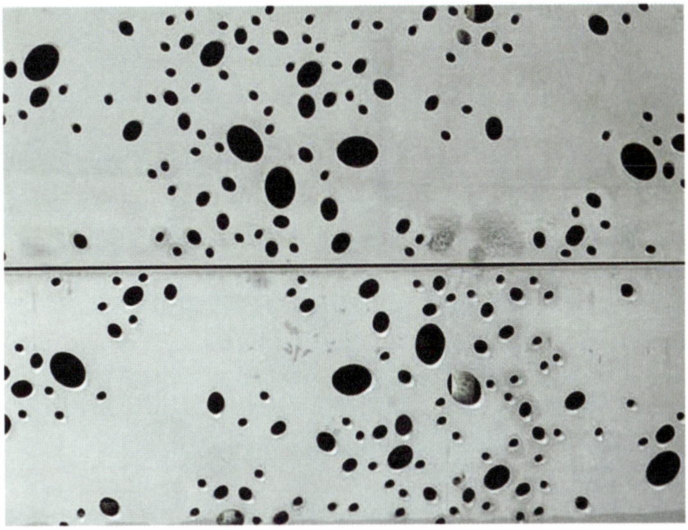

"For us it was very important to deal with that new façade. The façade has to relate to the old building and also to the mountain. With the local artists Leopoldo Ferrán and Agustina Otero we walked around the mountain Urgull and we saw the situation in which the stones were eroded by the wind, by the sea. At the same time we saw that there were those plants that were coming out of these holes in the stones, and we decided to try to translate this situation into our building. So we worked on prefabricated aluminum panels that were going to be perforated by holes through which the vegetation was going to come out. The façade was developed with five different panels. The most perforated panel has up to 260 holes. Of course, we were not looking for something like the façade of the CaixaForum in Madrid. For us, the vegetation had to be low and not cover all of the façade. This is the situation with the façade: we have a wall, in front of which we have the panels held by a frame. This frame holds three of the aluminum panels, and behind them we have the specific material which holds the plants. Then we have a hydroponic solution that is connected to the irrigation system, so that the plants are fed when they are irrigated.

The plants were simply introduced by hand, because it was the easiest and most natural way to do it.

During the whole process of the construction, we were working with the panels and planting the vegetation. So we did experiments and learned how the plants behaved. In the end it worked very well and the plants grew by themselves. Of course the plants need maintenance and cutting and the green is completely controlled. From a distance the building is always seen as a simple volume, but when you get closer, you start to feel the depth of the façade and the different layers. During the night you see those different layers, in which some of the perforated elements are used for natural light inside the building. Other elements are used for artificial light that comes out during the night. At night the light is more evident than the plants, but during the day the plants merge with the mountain."

“Green does not make architecture better or worse; it depends on the situation and the concept. Nature cannot be a must. Nature must bring specific benefits in specific situations, both architecturally and ecologically.”

FUENSANTA NIETO

ARVO PÄRT CENTER
LAULASMAA, ESTONIA
2014–2018

The Arvo Pärt Center was founded in 2010 by Arvo Pärt, an important Estonian composer of new music, with the aim of preserving his creative heritage. The planned building is to be built on a peninsula with dense pine forest, 35 kilometers from Tallinn. Nieto Sobejano Arquitectos won the competition in 2014 with their concept which saved most of the trees on the property. The public and private rooms, connected in a flowing floor plan, are combined under a large roof with glass exterior walls. The center's program includes the actual archive, a library, rooms for workshops, offices, and exhibition rooms, and an auditorium for concerts, performances, conferences and films.

"When we entered the site of the competition, the first thing we saw was this beautiful place. When somebody says you have to build here, it is very difficult because the nature here is absolutely impressive. There are pine trees, in different dimensions of course, but all of them are higher than 25 meters. So we proposed a project in which we could save the maximum number of trees we could, even though we knew that we had to build the building. What we suggested for this project was really like a floating roof. A floating roof that, through its form and its shape, was going to be able to adapt to the maximum number of trees—and at the same time, it was going to be perforated with patios that were going to act as vases inside the building. All the vases hold the trees that are inside the roof. For Arvo Pärt the silences in the music are very important, and we tried to relate that silence in the music to the voids in the building. We tried to work for nature, trying not to disrupt it and to save as many trees as we could. The facade follows one of the rhythms of the music of Arvo Pärt and, of course, it's very open. And there's this other element, a tower, that we wanted to push over the trees, because Arvo Pärt had the desire to see the sea, which is very nearby. It was developed according to the Fibonacci series and it's really only an elevator and stairs that take him to the rooftop, where he can sit and see the sea."

"For the Arvo Pärt Center in the forest of Lo Lasma, we wanted to integrate as many trees as possible. In this way, the building is a floating roof that is perforated to accommodate the trees. The trees are more important than the building. Silences in the music are like the voids in the building." FUENSANTA NIETO

GREEN POWER

JACOB VAN RIJS is one of the three founders of the Dutch architecture practice MVRDV, which incorporates green architecture but not necessarily as a central focus. Nonetheless, many of their avant-garde projects emerging over the last twenty years have been strongly linked to nature, greenery, and sustainability. One of the most respected buildings is certainly the Dutch pavilion of Expo 2000, which—with its construction of stacked landscapes including a forest—gave the office its reputation as forward-thinking. One of the largest MVRDV projects with a reference to nature is yet to come: the gardening fair Floriade 2022 in Almere, a model for the green city of the future.

1

JACOB VAN RIJS: "With Torre Huerta we tried to show a building that is absorbing the countryside; agricultural plots are flipped and more or less become a façade of the building. This was social housing: straight and efficient, good floor plans, the only special feature being balconies with trees—and trees that give food.

Luc Sigon, our French graphic designer, told us about an effect they also use in their image making. They call it the 'happiness filter.' You can make any building, any projects look good with greenery by just putting the happiness filter over it. It's a kind of really strange marketing phenomena. The green—the green effect, the happiness filter—is a powerful tool that any architect knows about.

Architecture is not always appreciated but the plants are. No one is against green so green is the way!"

2

1 Has green become a religion? **2** The happiness filter, Luxigon **3** 3D Garden, MVRDV **4** Torre Huerta, MVRDV

"Sometimes you make a house with a big balcony so that, instead of having all the houses next to each other eat up a lot of space, you can make one compact building and leave the rest empty. This mixture of urbanity and landscape will become an even bigger issue as cities get bigger. It has been a dream of ours to have this integration of gardening in architecture for a long time."

JACOB VAN RIJS

3

4

NETHERLANDS PAVILION AT THE 2000 WORLD EXPO
HANNOVER, 2000

Under the motto "Holland creates space", the Dutch pavilion at the 2000 World Expo in Hanover presented a possible way of dealing with limited space by piling six Dutch landscapes on top of each other in a built structure as independent ecosystems. The radical architecture, including a forest inside the building, as a motiv of an open, progressive society is combined with traditional values and stereotypes such as tulips, windmills, and dykes.

"The most important thing to try out was actually to put a forest in the building, and to put stuff on top of each other that is normally next to each other in the building. For the forest, we had to grow the trees in a kind of box. In order to do that, we had to do it in advance, because these trees were coming from a plantation and one year before the Expo opened, they were already in a box. Then the winter came and the summer came and then they were transported to Hannover into the building in little crates so they could survive. Some are still alive. Others have died in the meantime.

We made this little forest, lit by fluorescent tubelights and a reflective ceiling. If you were brought there with a blindfold you could have the illusion that you were in a forest. That was the goal that we wanted to reach, at least for this element in the project."

"The Expo Pavilion is a good example. It deals with the fact that there is too much—let's say—crowdedness in the country, but where we say that by putting things together, this forest in the building has the effect of creating some space elsewhere. It is literally a notion on urbanism." JACOB VAN RIJS

NTR, OFFICES

HILVERSUM, 1995–1997

The NTR building is part of a "campus" of cooperating television companies, which together form the third public television channel in the Netherlands.

By partly pushing the one-story office building into a hill and designing the visible roof surfaces with greenery, it blends with the landscape depending on the angle of view.

"Sometimes, it is interesting to use greenery and vegetation to hide a building ... We had a beautiful green plot where we wanted to build a one-story office building which you should not be able to see from the street. So, we managed to get the confirmation even though it was not in the building zoning regulations."

GWANGGYO POWER CENTER

SEOUL, 2008

MVRDV emerged as the winner of a developer competition in 2008 with its plan for a dense city within the future city of Gwanggyo, 35 kilometers south of the Korean capital Seoul. The concept envisages a series of buildings of different uses, which formally refer to a green, Korean hillside landscape. The so-called "Power Center" of the new city was designed to achieve programmatic diversity within urban density accompanied by a demand for sustainability.

"To our surprise this made it into TIME magazine as one of the most green buildings. We were never really aiming for that, and some of the people started to say 'hey, but these guys are just greenwashers'. You know, they just put some plants on the buildings to make it look more sustainable."

GROWING GREEN CITIES
FLORIADE ALMERE
OOSTERWORLD, 2022

In the course of the Floriade, a decennial international garden show in the Netherlands, MVRDV have developed a strategy for Almere, the location of the upcoming Floriade 2022. The design concept aims to raise awareness of simple, everyday plants and trees and translates this understanding into an urban landscape that creates architecture and urbanity, one which comprehends nature as an integral part: "free design and construction will transform an area of 43 square kilometers. Limits are set to ensure the rural character of the area is maintained: 18% construction, 8% roads, 13% public green space, 2% water and 59% urban agriculture. An individual's creativity is limitless within this framework."

"The Floriade is, of course, a piece of the city—and it shows the connection of plants and what plants can do. So, it's kind of an exposition, like the World Expo, but for plants. It should be combining energy—it should be autonomous in that sense—but it also should be a place to live and to stay, so that it's not only for plants and animals, but also for people in the future. At the beginning it's a theme park, but it can be transformed into a neighborhood.

So this is the dream we have—Almere is changing from a Garden City into a kind of green city, the future of the Garden City, so to say."

"The idea is to reflect the city in the lake, in which you would see the horticultural exhibition. Like a *fata morgana* reflected in the polder that will slowly turn into green."

JACOB VAN RIJS

BIOSPHERE 3

For the artist and trained architect TOMÁS SARACENO, green is not just a color but a way to take care. His work is often strongly influenced by climate change and population growth. Recurrent motifs are three-dimensional, often floating spatial structures, which, in addition to researching new forms of living and habitation, are also explicitly designed as a green space in the form of gardens or greenhouses.

BIOSPHERE 3

TOMÁS SARACENO: "The term biosphere refers to the zone of a planet in which life occurs. It is a closed, largely self-regulating system that integrates all living creatures and their relationships. As Richard Buckminster Fuller said: 'Our spaceship (Earth) is so superbly designed as to be able to keep life regenerating on board despite the phenomenon, entropy, by which all local physical systems lose energy. So we have to obtain our biological life-regenerating energy from another spaceship, the sun.'"

The building complex Biosphere 2, built in Arizona in 1991, attempted to show that it is possible to create a self-sustaining ecosystem, similar to the biosphere, independent of the outside world. The experiment was stopped after two unsuccessful attempts.

Tomás Saraceno's Biosphere 3 is based on his installation project Cloud Cities, which designed several often geodesic structures, which were to enable people to live in the upper atmosphere. As a long-term research project, the aim is to develop modular, transnational, and self-regulating cities. The structures floating in the clouds are supposed to contain whole ecosystems including lakes and forests.

"I was thinking about the flying garden in relation to Buckmister Fuller: Planet Earth as Biosphere 1 and the biggest garden in which we are living today, Biosphere 2 as the experiment done in the 70s in Arizona, and Biosphere 3, which I am trying to work on. Just to give you the scale, context, and the scope of my work when talking about the flying garden: Planet Earth is flying already—or Spaceship Earth as Bucky would say."

1

2

3

1 Planet Earth **2** Biosphere 2 Arizona **3** Biosphere 3, Collage, Studio Tomás Saraceno 2015

1

"We need to change the way we travel, communicate, and inhabit the planet—climate change makes rethinking inequalities very urgent."

TOMÁS SARACENO

2

"It is mostly about the relationships involved in something turning green. It's not only about color but also the way and intention of becoming green, and thinking about how we can take care of something… then maybe we can call it Hortitecture."

TOMÁS SARACENO

1 *60SE Flying Garden/Air-Port-City*, Studio Tomás Saraceno, 2006
2 *32SW/Stay green/Flying Garden/Air-Port-City*, Studio Tomás Saraceno, 2007–2009

URBAN BIODIVERSITY & ECOSYSTEM SERVICES

Urban areas are heterogeneous and dynamic ecosystems with interacting human and natural processes. BORIS SCHRÖDER-ESSELBACH and STEPHAN WEBER from the Institute of Geoecology focus on urban biodiversity and ecosystems services.

1

2

STEPHAN WEBER: "As an urban climatologist I am interested how the buildings in the city with many different surface materials affect the climate. We normally think about planting on ground soil, but here we really have the chance to think about having green where no green was before.

If we think about ecosystem services in mitigating climate change, buildings that multipy the surface of plants have a strong capability for filtering the air and absorbing carbon.

Urban ecosystems are characterised by specific environmental conditions: vegetation is replaced by sealed surfaces, and soils are degraded and compacted. Thus, infiltration of water decreases and groundwater formation is reduced, but stormwater runoff and peak flow increase. Evapotranspiration is also reduced, and urban runoff increases eutrophication. The urban heat island effect increases air temperature by a couple of degrees Celsius, e.g. 2-8°, so that snow cover and the duration of frost periods is reduced and the vegetation period is prolonged. Levels of air pollution (e.g. particulate matter and nitrogen dioxide) are considerably higher compared to the rural surroundings. Disturbances change due to light pollution, trampling, elevated noise levels, etcetera.

BORIS SCHRÖDER-ESSELBACH: "Urban biodiversity is the variety and richness of living organisms and habitats in human settlements, ranging from the rural fringe to the city centers. The specific cocktail of environmental conditions and their strong heterogeneity makes for novel urban ecosystems not experienced by many species before. Some pre-adapted species (such as foxes, wild boars, bed bugs, peregrine falcons, and other synanthropic species) benefit from these novel ecosystems because of adaptations in diets and behaviour. Hence, some winners replace many losers. On a global scale, we can observe a decrease in biodiversity, but on a local scale an increase, particularly of non-native species. Considering species loss in rural areas due to industrial agriculture, forestry and climate change is driving species out of natural reserves. Urban regions, therefore, can also be understood as refuges for the remnants of our biodiversity."

3

Biodiversity
- number
- relative abundance
- composition
- interactions

→

Ecosystem services / ESS

Provisioning of
- food and goods
- genetic resources

Support of
- habitat
- water-/nutrient cycling
- soil formation

Regulation of
- climatic extremes
- noise reduction
- air purification
- disease, pests ...

Cultural services
- recreation, aesthetic benefits
- cognitive development
- place values & social cohesion

↓

Ecosystem functions
- production
- regulation
- habitat

→

1 + 2 The roof of the new airport in Berlin
3 Millenium Ecosystem Assessment: Ecosystems and Human well-being-biodiversity synthesis, Source: Elmqvist T et al. (Eds.). 2013. *Urbanization, Biodiversity and Ecosystem Services.*

1

1 GIS analysis of green roof potential in Braunschweig
2 Services of urban green roofs and the results on the urban scale

"Ecosystem services are what nature provides us for free. They are strongly related to human well-being. An urban tree, for instance, produces O^2, absorbs CO^2, reduces temperature extremes, filters and absorbs pollutant gases including ozone, sulphur dioxide, carbon monoxide, and nitrogen dioxide, reduces noise and dust levels, and provides wildlife habitat—to name just a couple of benefits. Ecosystem services in general are classified into supporting services (e.g. soil formation), provisioning services (e.g. food, fibers, clean water, and cooling), regulating services (e.g. clean air, water purification, and carbon storage), as well as cultural services (e.g. recreation, education, and aesthetic and spiritual values).

Green infrastructure provides substantial benefits to biodiversity and human well-being in urban regions by providing a range of ecosystem services. This holds for the buildings scale, which is the focus of the Hortitecture approach, as well as for plants on the urban scale.

To promote healthy and sustainable cities we should use nature to minimize health risks through the reduction of environmental stressors (e.g. air pollution and noise) as well as by optimizing health resources providing nature experience, social contacts, sporting activity, recreation and relaxation.

In our research, we focus on modelling and quantifying ecosystem services by measurements. This is the basis for analysing trade-offs and synergies and for comparing the current ecological state of urban systems with scenarios for potential developments. With such an analysis, we provide a valuable instrument to support planning tools for sustainable urban development."

"In my eyes architecture could relate to knowledge on ecological patterns and processes, could relate to the knowledge that we gain provisionning eco system services ... a good architect should relate to this knowledge, which is gained in the scientific community."

BORIS SCHRÖDER ESSELBACH

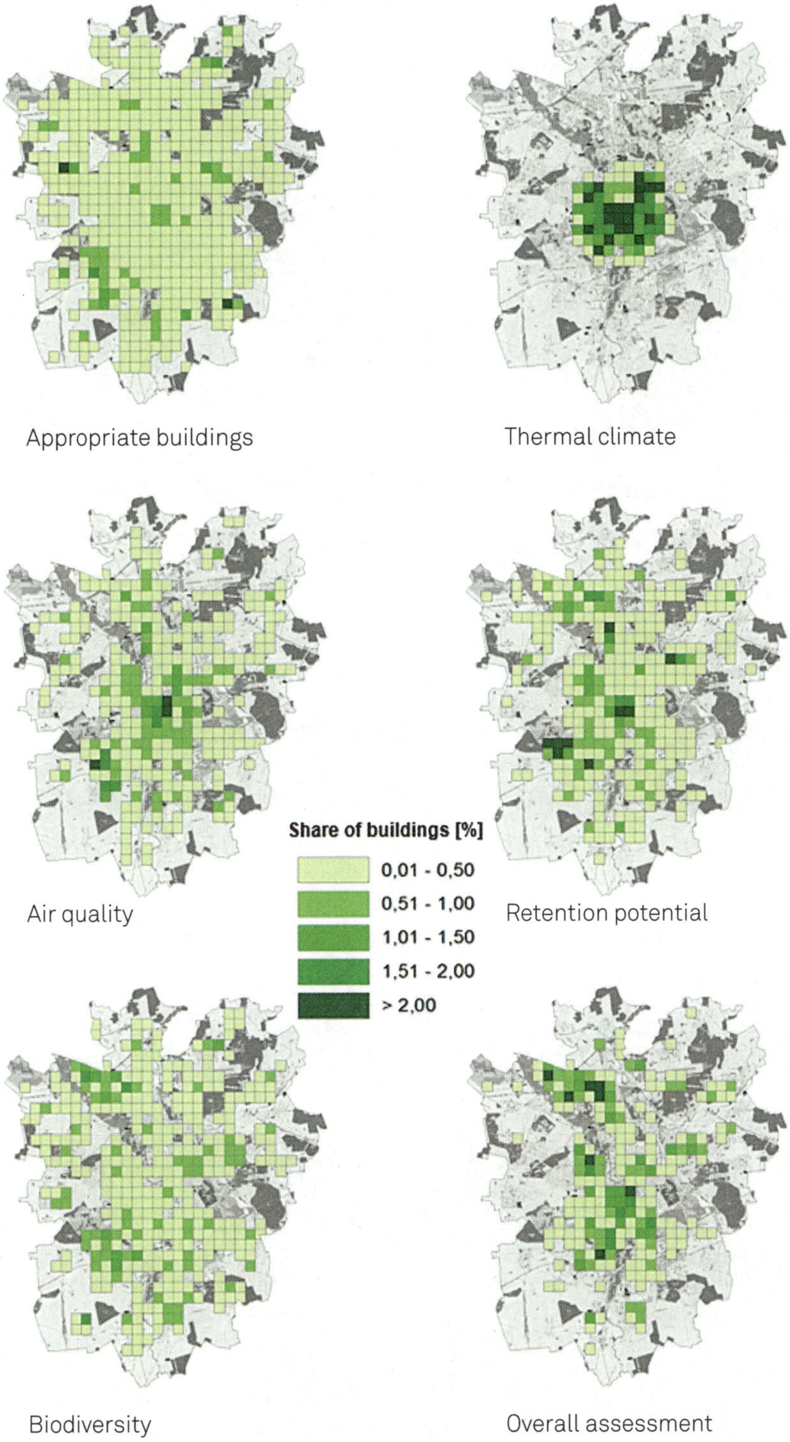
Appropriate buildings
Thermal climate
Air quality
Retention potential
Share of buildings [%]
0,01 - 0,50
0,51 - 1,00
1,01 - 1,50
1,51 - 2,00
> 2,00
Biodiversity
Overall assessment

GROWTH AS A CONCEPT

Constructing Architecture directly with living trees is the main aim of FERDINAND LUDWIG and DANIEL SCHÖNLE. Inspired by historic examples like the *Tanzlinden* or living root bridges, their office deals with the spatial, aesthetic, ecological, constructive, and processual potentials of trees in architecture, urban development, and open-space planning. This work is grounded on foundational research by the Research Group Baubotanik at the University of Stuttgart now continued at the Technical University of Munich.

"We try to merge the world of building with the world of growing, especially the growth of trees. There are historic examples for this approach, like the so-called *Tanzlinden*, for example in Peesten, Bavaria. A grown tree was formed to create a canopy with an integrated dance floor. In India, people have been using grafting techniques to form bridges for several hundred years. These living bridges may look like a kind of a fairy-tale, but it's a real engineering approach (Ref. Middleton). They have spans of more than twenty meters and can hold dozens of people, and the loadbearing structure is completely constructed from tree roots. The natural phenomena that are used for our architecture are first of all natural inosculation, which can occur when two branches, trunks, or roots come into contact and then merge. The second phenomenon is the incorporation of technical, non-living elements that are incorporated by the tree during the growth process."

"In our projects trees really are an integral part of building, a part of the construction and thus the architecture itself—the building begins to act like a tree."

LUDWIG SCHÖNLE

FERDINAND LUDWIG: "For my PhD, I worked on these inosculation techniques to really transform this horticultural practice into something that is applicable in architecture and building. We experimented with hundreds; I think in the end it was eight hundred trees, of about ten different species. We did a lot of tests to develop techniques that really work when you make structures based on this approach. When you make cross-sections through these inosculated branches you see something very interesting: it is not only that you do something like 'welding wood,' you merge one or even more organisms into one. In the beginning we have two plants, and then it's only one—because both are sharing all the nutrition, all the water and everything they produce by photosynthesis."

DANIEL SCHÖNLE: "We developed a technique that we often use in our projects now; we call it the plant addition technique. We use several hundred—sometimes up to thousand or even more—plants, and we join them together so that they inosculate. We only plant some in the ground, the others are planted in special pots in some kind of scaffolding and then we connect them and let them merge. The merged structure sucks up the water from the ground, where they get the most, and then we can cut away the containers and we have created one artificial tree that we can form and give a certain structure. In the beginning we need a watering system, of course, but in the end it is as strong and as resilient as a naturally grown tree."

1

2

3

4

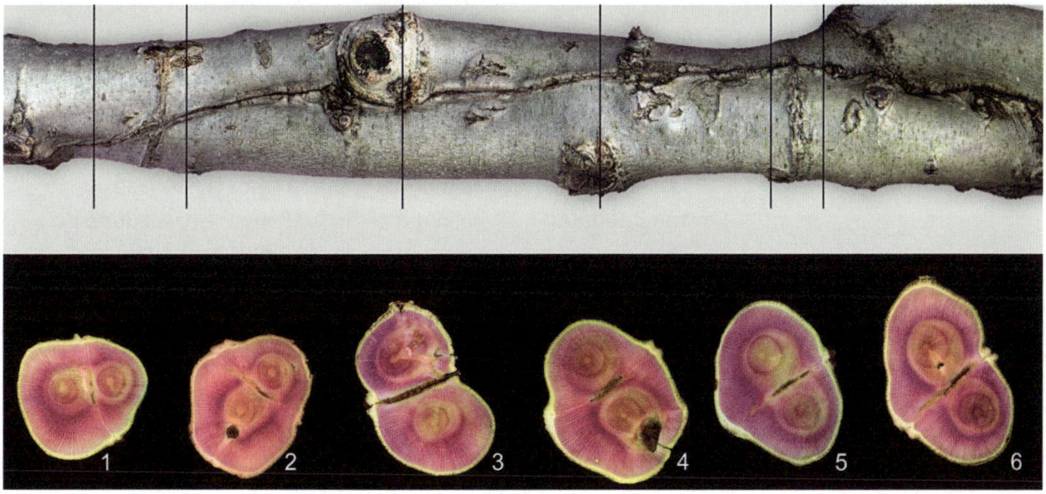

5

1 *Tanzlinden*, Peesten **2** Living bridges, India **3** Natural inosculation **4** Incorporation of Technical Elements **5** Cross sections through inosculated branches

BAUBOTANIK TOWER
WALD-RUHESTETTEN, GERMANY, 2009

FERDINAND LUDWIG: "The Baubotanik Tower in Wald-Ruhestetten, realized in 2009, was our first step into really building and designing with trees as a part of the building process and structure. What we made was a very simple, temporary scaffolding. We put some plant containers in it and arranged around 400 young plants in this big structure to create the load-bearıng structure of the future. We built up the treebuilding with a crane in four days until we reached 8 meters. After that we connected the plants with screws. Even though gardeners wouldn't support it, it is a very simple technique to make the plants join and work as one. Then we just let it grow.

What we normally call 'completion' is never finished, of course. We are now cutting off the roots in the pots, and stepbystep the plants will suck up the water from the ground. At the moment we still have a watering system in the container, but we will not need it in the future. What we learned with this project is that we always have to think in different scenarios. We are not sure how it will look in two years, in five years, in ten years, or in fifteen years."

PLANE TREE CUBE
NAGOLD, GERMANY, 2012

DANIEL SCHÖNLE: "Our second step into realising the idea of living architecture is more or less comparable, the so-called Plane Tree Cube, Platanenkubus, which we made for a garden exhibition *(Landesgartenschau)* in southern Germany in 2012. It is more or less the same system as the Baubotanik Tower, but it is the first one that was done for a public space. It will be a kind of 'public tree' with three levels to walk on, and is part of the city development as a vertical square for the future. What we had to do as architects, engineers, and designers was really very precise planning, of course. The trees had to be part of the whole building process, they had to be part of the technical construction and its timeline. Our answer was a Baubotanik prefabrication system, where we prearranged, in this case, four plants in one pot, and already connected them so that they started to inosculate. Then (just using a crane) we attached them to this partly permanent, partly temporary structure, connected them to the water-dripping system and let them connect with the neighbouring plants so that they could merge into one. In this case, around 1,200 plants are now merging into one big tree organism."

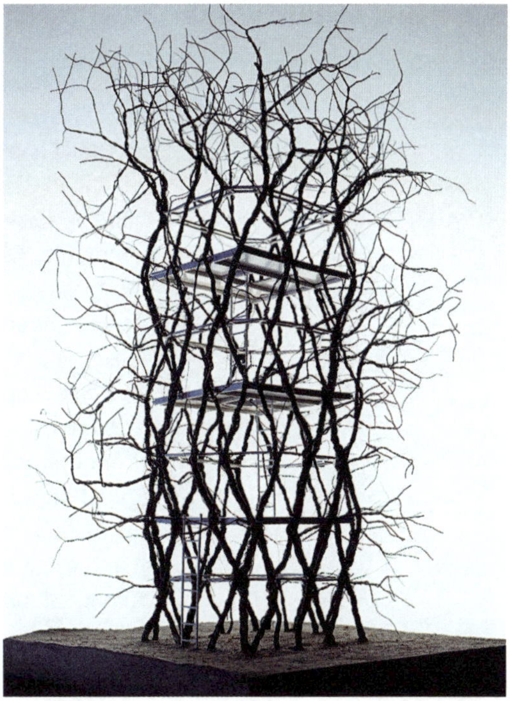

"We use hundreds or even more plants, joining them together in such a way that they inosculate. Thereby, we create an artificial tree that we can form to generate the specific structure that we want to have." LUDWIG SCHÖNLE

HOUSE OF THE FUTURE
COMPETITION, 2011

"The competition 'House of the Future' in Berlin asked for the creation of a kind of museum that should exhibit the design and techniques of the future. Since no-one knows what this will look like, we decided to suggest a building of which we also don't know what it will look like in the future—due to its tree facade. Though we got the third prize we were very much criticized by some jury members and the architectural community. As an architect, you have to design the appearance of the building and you should not give it up to a plant, many architects or colleagues told us. But we tried to design it like this and we tried really to design a hybrid that is, on the same plot, a building with 10,000 square meters of usable space and a tree. In order to do this, you even have to reinvent the way you draw. Normally, we have the figure-ground plan in black for the urban structure and we have the green surrounding it. Here it's all mixed, so we also have to find a new way of drawing and representing it. The basic concept of the building was a solid block in the middle. Then we have the exhibition areas, which enclose the core, moving up step-by-step. They are accessed by a spiralling ramp with a tree-and-glass façade. If you go through the building, through the exhibition spaces, you have, every time you step out on this ramp, a great view through the canopy over the city of Berlin. One important aspect for us are these atmospheric and spatial potentials. The other is, at the same time and at the same level, the ecological benefit of Baubotanik architecture, because trees—as we all know—have these benefits of shading, of heat reduction, of cooling the air by evaporation and filtering the air, removing fine dust, and so on. The client really was concerned about the wildness of natural growth. This is somehow understandable, because humans and plants are somehow in competition for light and space, but you can react to this—e.g. with the right choice of an appropriate plant species and maintenance concept. Together with the company Transsolar, we developed a concept for this building where we harvest the rain on the sealed surfaces, bringing it back to the tree. That way the tree can grow in the city, acting as a kind of air conditioning system for the building and its environment. Here we see a substantial difference to the so-called passive house architecture. These are normally 'stupid boxes,' looking only inside and reflecting all the heat into the urban environment, whereas Baubotanik architecture also improves the public space. So it's somehow inbetween open space and building design, and thus should be realized through close collaboration of architects and landscape architects, bringing these two different fields closer together."

"The core of our work is uncertainty and process. So for the 'House of the Future' we wanted to work with the idea of un-determinedness by building a house as a tree—a house that grows towards the future." BAUBOTANIK

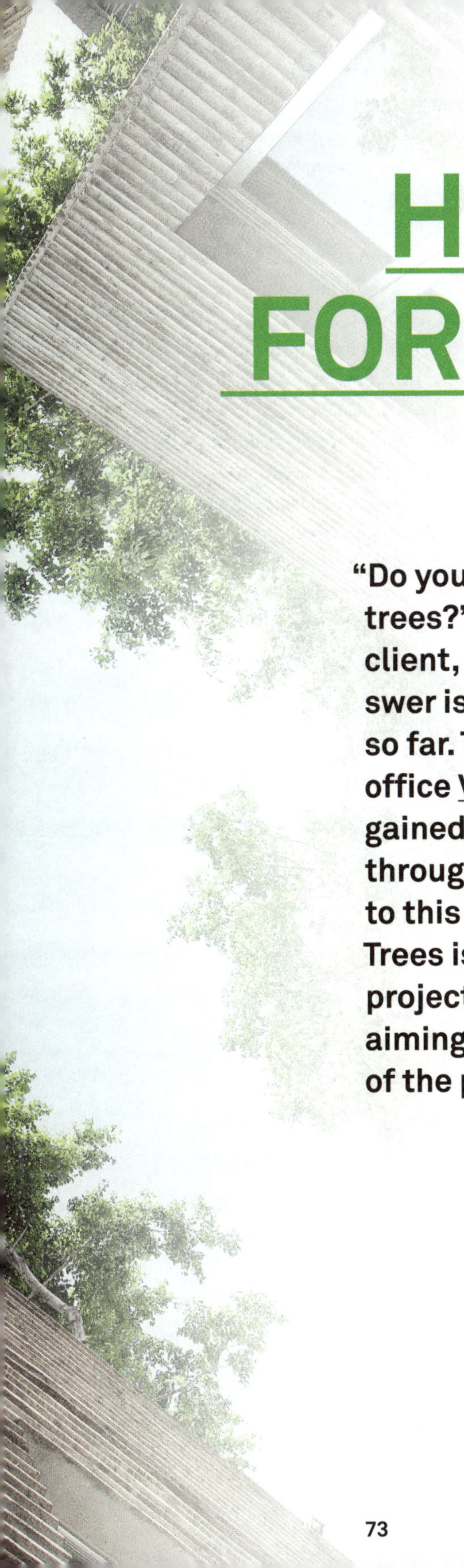

HOUSES FOR TREES

"Do you want to build a house for trees?" VO TRONG NGHIA asks every client, and refuses the job if the answer is no, which has not happened so far. The Vietnamese architecture office VO TRONG NGHIA ARCHITECTS gained international recognition through a project directly connected to this initial question—House for Trees isn't just the name for one project, but for a series of projects aiming at intensifying the greening of the planet.

VO TRONG NGHIA: "This is the situation in Ho Chi Minh City. We just have 0.7 square meters of green per person. You can compare it to Bangkok, Beijing, Kuala Lumpur, Hong Kong, Singapore, or Tokyo. We have a very big problem with lacking green in the city. We have a lot of pollution, floods, and overheating. We are in a tropical climate totally different from in German; we have summer the whole year. And last but not least, our population is increasing. As a reaction to these problems, our policy is to bring back green space into the city. I think if the situation does not improve, people will go crazy very soon. Now, 75% of the children in the city are inactive. So we need to have more and more green space. That is why I am doing a lot of houses for trees, and also a school building that provides shade. Furthermore, we have an electricity shortage. In summertime, the electricity stops every day. If we had enough shade and big trees shading the glass windows, you could just open these big windows. The power for the entire university costs a lot and that is the reason why we have to plant trees."

"Building a house, a piece of architecture, is just a device on which to plant a tree … The main purpose is to plant a tree to green our cities and green our earth" VO TRONG NGHIA

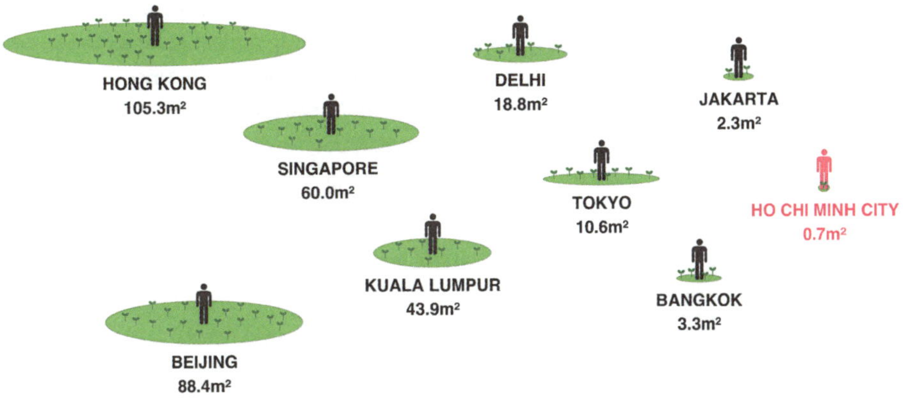

EAST ASIAN AVERAGE

66.2m^2 / person

HO CHI MINH CITY

0.7m^2 / person

> **"For a modern architect, the most important mission is to bring green spaces back to the Earth."** VO TRONG NGHIA

HOUSE FOR TREES
HO CHI MINH CITY, VIETNAM, 2014

With a budget of only US $150,000, the House for Trees is designed as five freestanding buildings of exposed concrete of different heights, which accommodate various residential functions. At the same time, they each serve as a kind of oversized pot, as birch figs grow on the roofs, providing shade, serving as stormwater-management, and improving the microclimate.

"We designed the House For Trees, which is a house for depressed people, like a pot for a tree. We planted fifteen really big trees on it, ficus trees, which get big very fast and now cover the whole building. We needed to make the depressed people active because they are inactive people due to their disease. Therefore, we designed a lot of green spaces that make the people active. Somehow this new relation should be factored into the interaction between architects and landscape architects, bringing these two different fields closely together.

We used local materials to realize a low-cost housing project. The House for Trees is not only one house, but a city of houses. We ask any client who comes to us: Do you want to build a House for Trees? And if they say no we refuse to do the job. We only want to accept jobs that are meaningful for us, to use our resources as efficiently as possible.

This is the first project where we planted really big trees on the houses. We don't have any green in the city so this kind of roof retains a lot of water. In Ho Chi Minh City we have floods almost every day because it rains so much and the sea level is rising. We need to do something like this to keep the water on site, rather than letting it flood the city. This is a ficus and this tree already almost covers the whole house. Using a tree as a shading device is really low cost in tropical climates. It costs just $200, and if you plant ten trees like this it costs just $2000."

0 1 2 5m

FARMING KINDERGARTEN
DONGNAI,
VIETNAM, 2013

The kindergarten, which is designed for 500 children from a nearby shoe factory, serves, in addition to its childcare-function, as a training center for sustainability and is intended to enable children to develop a relationship with nature. The building is equipped with a continuous walkable green roof in the form of three band-like ellipses, which offer space for experimental vegetable gardens.

"Because the children don't have a lot of playgrounds and a lot of green space in Vietnam, we maximized the activity space for the children with a continuous roof. The workers come to grow the vegetables for the children's lunch every day. And the children can learn a lot from them about agriculture, and the families are encouraged to join in and to grow the vegetables on the roof. The kindergarten also provides a gym and a kitchen. On the upper floor we can find the music room and the office, and all these functions are covered by the continuous green roof. The vertical connection between the different floors and between the ground floor and the roof is both by staircase and slope. Two classrooms share one bathroom. Because the budget of this building was really limited, we used mainly passive design methods to climatize the building—like solar water heaters, green façades, louvers, and recycled water from the factory. Furthermore, we kept the existing trees as natural shading devices. The classrooms are simply cooled by operable windows and deep eaves to protect from the sunlight. We don't use any air conditioning for the classrooms. It is really easy to use the wind to cool the buildings and classrooms, but to make sure that every classroom is cooled efficiently by cross ventilation we had to simulate it so that we knew how to open the windows. The louvers and the green façade protect from the sunlight. These kinds of trees grow really fast and now they cover the whole courtyard. In our country we have heavy rains and we use the recycled wastewater from the factory to irrigate the greenery in the rooftop garden. The whole construction costs for the building was only US$1,900,000."

"Factory workers' kids can learn about agriculture through rooftop farming." VO TRONG NGHIA

STACKING GREEN
HO CHI MINH CITY, VIETNAM, 2011

Extremly narrow houses are typical in Vietnamese cities. Vo Trong Nghia Architects realized one of them in Hanoi and called it Stacking Green. Vertical layered plants in the façade create the special atmosphere within the building.

"A special feature of this very narrow house, which is only 4 meters wide and 20 meters deep, is the front facade. Horizontally layered concrete planters with an integrated irrigation system fed by rainwater enable a green façade that protects against sunlight, noise, and pollution, and makes an otherwise indispensable air-conditioning system superfluous. The roof garden protects the interior from the heat by strong sunlight."

"In Europe, a double skin is defined by three layers: Glass—Air—Glass. But, in a tropical climate it should be defined as Green—Air—Glass."

VO TRONG NGHIA

NATURE-CITY

Although often associated with the idea of efficiency, sustainability, and performance, the interesting aspect of green buildings for DAN WOOD is more in how plants can become an integrated part of a building. As co-founder of the New York-based Architecture Company WORKac, which achieved recognition for projects reinventing the relationship between buildings and nature, his work focuses on the intersection between the urban, the rural, and the wild.

EDIBLE SCHOOLYARDS
NEW YORK, 2010

The Edible Schoolyard initiative was launched in 1995 by Alice Waters in a vacant lot at the Martin Luther King Jr. Middle School, Berkeley. The concept includes a kind of gardening-and-kitchen-classroom.

DAN WOOD: "Edible Schoolyard teaches elementary-school children how to grow and to cook food, and integrates that completely within the curriculum. So they're also learning about mathematics, history, science, and art, all through the medium of food. We built the first one in New York City and this is becoming a major new curriculum item in education. We don't have as much space as as in Berkeley but we basically reclaim parts of the parking lot here and transform that first into a kind of incredibly productive landscape.

And it's very true, at least for children, that if they grow it and cook it they are going to eat it. It's very amazing to watch the kids get excited about kale salad.

The building itself combines a greenhouse, a kitchen classroom, and this kind of visible sustainable infrastructure at the back, which is the chicken coop, the water cistern, water-collecting system, and the air conditioning and the composting toilet are also kind of expressed. Everything is combined together but expressed separately. So water that falls on the greenhouse roof then joins water falling on the classroom roof and it's collected in the cistern in the back and then reused as irrigation for the plants."

"Sustainability is not just about efficiency; it's about changing people's attitudes, and by introducing nature in unexpected places we can make people think differently about living in the city. When you say 'green building,' you think of efficiency, sustainability, and buildings that perform in a certain way. What is really different and interesting about Hortitecture is that plants and animals become an integrative part of the building." DAN WOOD

PUBLIC FARM 1
NEW YORK, 2008

In the course of the yearly Young Architects Program (YAP) competition, WORKac was able to realize its concept of Public Farm 1 at the MoMa PS1 in 2008.

"The requirements for the temporary pavilion in the courtyard of the P1 in Queens were shade, seeding, and water. We decided to celebrate the fortieth anniversary of 1968—this was in 2008—by kind of reimagining what kind of future the city could have and we came up with the idea of an urban farm that sponsored a kind of infrastructure for parties underneath it.

It was completely built out of cardboard tubes with fifty-two kinds of fruits and vegetables growing at the top. We used primarily reclaimed rainwater from the roof of the museum. It was all solar powered—from the pumps to get the water up to even the blender for making cocktails out of vegetables. It got up to 10 meters tall at its highest point. At the end, it was completely disassembled and recycled back into paper..."

In 2009, WORKac published the book *49 Cities*, the quintessence of a research project exploring urban models from the Roman ideal city to the utopias of the twentieth century and comparing their programs with regard to density, efficiency and amount of green area.

"*49 Cities* was really going back and looking at the history of urbanism. We looked at 200 projects and narrowed it down to forty-nine—and looked at them comparatively through what we call the green lens. Each of these projects was analyzed in terms of its floor area ratio; its amount of green space. For example, we looked at Ebenezer Howard 's Garden City of 1901. The relationship became very clear between the green productive spaces where there were cows and cattle and farmyards, and the development of the city itself in the middle. There was a really intrinsic relationship that was spelled out economically, culturally, and—also—we have figured out the amount of space required to build these cities.

At the end of the book, we chose the winning city. The one that performed the highest, had the most amount of people with the highest amount of density and the most amount of green space, and actually Radiant City was the winner. Then we went back and looked at Radiant City through this lens of green and really rediscovered things. For example, this is an illustration that Le Corbusier published saying this is what the open spaces of our great cities might be like, which is certainly not what we think of when we think of Le Corbusier and towers in the park. It's a much more interesting nuanced wild view of what the nature and city could be. We all know about his obsession with sports and sports fields, but the proposal in residential areas also had an enormous section devoted to urban farming. So that every resident was given a 20 square meter of farm plot to work. The protégé, which is here, had almost the exact same importance in the scheme as the residential projects and the sports fields. So this really opened our eyes to the possibilities of urbanism and really thinking through cities not just in terms of their built, their urban, environment but also with their relationship with the outside world and green space."

1

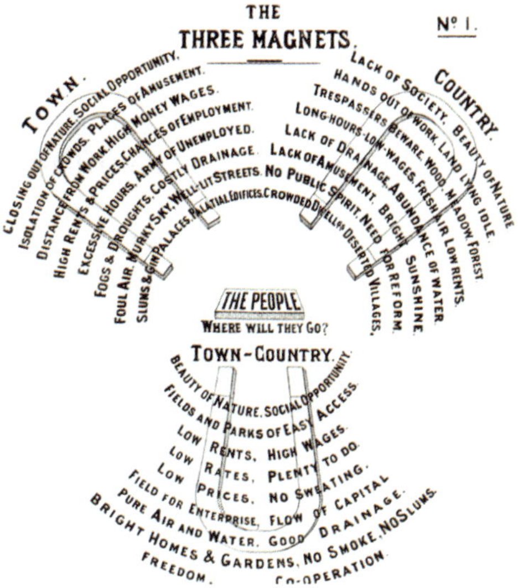

2

“Our book *49 Cities* opened our eyes to the possibilities of urbanism and thinking through cities not only with regards to their built environment but also in their relationship with the outside world and surrounding green spaces.” DAN WOOD

1 *49 Cities*, WORKac **2** “The Three Magnets.” Plate No. 1 from Ebenezer Howard’s Garden Cities of Tomorrow, 1902

NATURE CITY
NEW YORK, 2012

Designed for the exhibition "Foreclosed: Re-Housing the American Dream" by the Museum of Modern Art, WORKac's theoretical project Nature-City questions how we can live sustainably and close to nature at the same time, and reinvents Ebenezer Howard's concept of the Town-Country, a classic feature of the Garden City, which combines the comforts of urban life with the health benefits and access to agriculture of rural life.

"For Nature-City we returned to Ebenezer Howard's Garden City. This is his famous diagram where he kind of lists all the things that are wrong with the nineteenth-century city, including pollution and labor conditions and smog and sewers and everything. But he also lists everything that's wrong with the nineteenth-century countryside, which includes lack of education, lack of advancement—like a real hardscrabble life. He was really the first one who postulated this idea that you could have both: the town and the country, where you would have basically the best of both worlds. But of course this became today's suburbs, which are really not the best of both worlds.

So we chose a site in Oregon on the edge of some of the best farmland in the world. As the city was experiencing growth, this suburb was experiencing growth and proposing to kind of tear up more farmland to expand. We wanted to take a look at how an alternative could be created, where we took this kind of major ugly retail space and tried to put all the projected 14,000 new residents within the confines of the existing suburbs.

The idea was these kinds of piers of these very dense, very mixed, very diverse urban conditions, mixed with a very rural, wild condition. We researched the land and what the native forests and landscape would've been. There was an existing body of water that had been dammed up by the retail development which really divides a kind of oak savanna from a Douglas fir forest. So, it has the potential to be a very rich ecosystem. These kind of urban piers, combined with the nature here, created a solution whereby we were able to provide both five times the typical density of the suburb, so you had five times as many people living on the same amount of land, while at the same time we also had three times as much open space. It is both much more urban and dense and more open and rural. It really, in a way, became that kind of idealized Town-Country. To provide the needed water

“I was invited to this event because of our love of nature. Nearly all our work deals with the relationship between the urban, the rural and the wild and the intersections between them.”

DAN WOOD

pressure we created an indoor waterfall, with turbines producing electricty. We also proposed a massive composting chamber with a dome to collect methane gas, and placed terraced housing around it, profiting from the excess heat through a heated pool on top.

We realized bridges between the piers so that the landscaping could continue, so that plants and animals could kind of wanderer unimpeded throughout this land. We did economic forecasts and priced out the whole thing. We also had a maintenance plan to really make sure that this could work. This would be a kind of shared public space for over 14,000 people living there—and then that public space was expanded on each of the more dense developments, so that there was a whole range of different types of green space provided: from the wide wild public green space to parks to private green space at the houses.”

ARCHITECTURAL PSYCHOLOGY

The psychologist NICOLA MOCZEK, co-founder of the Berlin-based institute PSY:PLAN, deals with the influence of architecture and environment on the human psyche. Regarding the effects of vegetation, she sees green buildings primarily as a health benefit, as nature helps people to recover physically and mentally.

NICOLA MOCZEK: "Environmental psychology is an interdisciplinary field focusing on the interplay between individuals and their surroundings. The field defines the term 'environment' broadly, encompassing natural environments, social settings, built environments, learning environments, and informational environments. Architectural psychology focuses on the interactions between humans and built environments; i.e., on how the environment affects its inhabitants and vice versa.

Recently there has been a surge in the number of green roofs and façades installed—not only in Europe—with advocation of their use by policy-makers as well as claims that they are aesthetically pleasing. But these claims rely on generalizations from different landscapes, raising concerns about their validity. There are only a few existing (psychological) studies on the effects of building-integrated vegetation on humans, most of them conducted under laboratory conditions with manipulated pictures and renderings and not in real-life settings. There are more studies on the positive impact of nature on human behaviour and well-being—i.e. in the context of housing, working, and learning environments. So we highly recommend further studies under real-life conditions.

In my eyes the kindergarten of Mr. Vo is a wonderful learning environment. There is strong evidence from many studies that children benefit strongly from green environments. And there is much more psychology in that project: the concepts of privacy, place attachment, health, and well-being. I believe that children will not only learn better in the building, but that they will also learn from the building.

For architects, planners, real estate managers, and designers, building integrated vegetation is highly attractive—and so it is attractive for environmental psychologists as well. In dense urban areas, 'green buildings' promise the qualities of nature and a sustainable lifestyle, and can show a high symbolic value, especially in transformational projects from industrial to every day use. They promote relaxing and recreational effects, good working and living environments, and the rise of nature awareness and place attachment. Existing projects show enormous economical effects, like the conversion of the High Line into a park."

High Line, New York City
in 2012

"Nature helps people to recover physically and mentally. Even an indirect experience of nature, like a view towards green, can show beneficial effects. Green buildings promote relaxing and recreational effects, raise nature awareness and place attachment, and have positive economical effects as well. In dense cities, green elements offer qualities of nature and they have more than only symbolic value in transformational projects." NICOLA MOCZEK

BIO-INTEGRATION

Since the early seventies, KEN YEANG has been working in the field of ecological architecture and urbanism, concurrently seeking to develop the theory of ecological design, seeking to derive architectural interpretation, and developing sub-systems and devices and in the work of his office, HAMZAH & YEANG. For the pioneer of a green architectural movement, the true value of a green building lies in its capabilities; to, besides creating a healthier microclimate, make people happy and give them a pleasurable environment.

Ken Yeang defines green building as the seamless and benign biointegration of humanity's built environment and its production systems with nature, being the ecosystems and the biosphere's biogeochemical cycles. Through his office, he is working to create buildings and masterplans as hybrid techno-biological living systems that seek to biointegrate synergistically with the natural environment.

<u>KEN YEANG:</u> "I started working and thinking about green design back in 1971. I wanted to rethink the way architects think about and do green design. I concluded that effective biointegration of the human-made with nature is the key. It occurred to me that in many ways, green design is similar to what doctors and surgeons do with prostheses or with orthodontics. Prosthetic arms, prosthetic hearts, prosthetic kneecaps and so forth are essentially artificial and synthetic items and appendages that are either physically attached or systemically connected to a host organism. The host organism in medical prosthesis is the human body, wherein everything depends on the effectiveness of this connectivity. If this connectivity is not successful and is ineffective, then either the host organism dies or fails or gets injured, or the prosthetic device breaks down. In the analogy, the equivalent to the prosthetic device is our buildings and our built environment. It is synthetic, artificial and human-made. So then what is the host organism to our built environment as prosthesis? The answer is obvious—it's the biosphere. The biosphere is the host organism to everything that we make and do. And so, achieving successful biointegration between our built environment and nature is the crux of ecological design. Biointegration can be achieved at three levels: physical, synthetic and temporal.

How can we physically, systemically, and temporally biointegrate our built environment with the natural environment in a seamless, benign way? An ecologist sees the earth as covered by a thin film called the biosphere, and within the biosphere are ecosystems that consist of communities of plants and animals acting together to form a whole. It is this holistic property that differentiates organisms from mechanical systems, where in the organism its whole is greater than the sum of its parts.

Further elaborating on the biological structure of the ecosystem, the ecosystem is defined as consisting of biotic constituents and abiotic constituents—like the organic and the inorganic—acting together to form a whole. Looking at our existing built environment, it is evident that what are we doing as architects is making built environments where everything is physical. Where are the organic constituents, besides us humans, the bacteria, and the little creatures like rats and insects in our buildings? How can we bring organic life and organic constituents into the built environment?

I started to map out the basic options, these being the centralized, dispersed, semi-dispersed, and intertwining patterns. An example of the centralized relationship is Manhattan island with its Central Park, where the biotic constituents are all concentrated into one location. The second is a dispersed, spotty relationship, such as in the Georgian squares of London. The third option a 'stepping stone' relationship where he biotic constituents are aligned in a 'stepping stones', relationship. For the ecologist, the most effective and ideal relationship between the biotic and the abiotic is one in which there is an ecological nexus, in a continuous intertwining link. This is the preferred pattern of relationships. In effect, in nature, everything is linked."

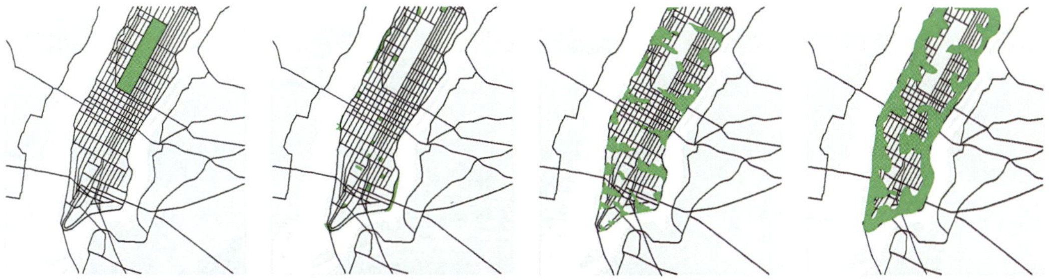

Centralized planting | Dispersed planting ('spotty' pattern) | Dispersed planting ('stepping stones') | Continous planting

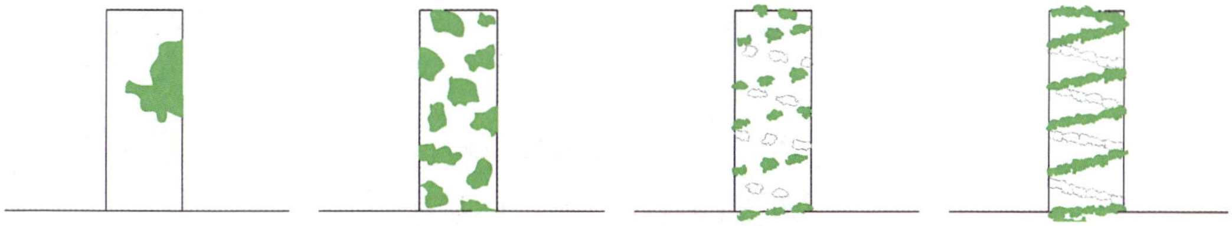

Juxtapositioning | Intermixing | Linear intermixing | Integrating

MENARA BOUSTEAD
KUALA LUMPUR, 1985

The Menara Boustead office building is designed as a bioclimatic passive energy-saving high-rise building. The façade allows for natural exposure on the north face, which does not get constant direct solar insolation. The other façades are recessed for solar protection, preventing excessive heating of the interior spaces. Vegetated skycourts as planted terraces are located at the edges to provide opportunities for natural ventilation spaces and to accommodate plants and green areas.

“The Boustead Tower is one of our early buildings (1985) where we put vegetation on the outside. This building's image is important for me, because it is emblematic of what an ecological aesthetic could look like. I believe that ecological architecture as green architecture deserves its own aesthetic. I think it should not be pristine, but appear 'hairy'.”

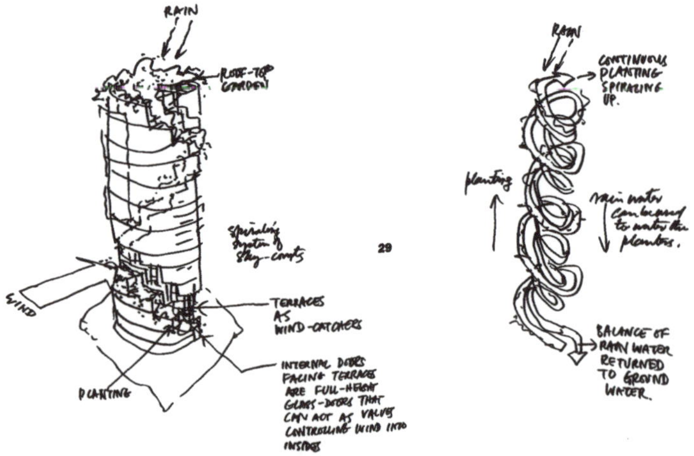

GENOME RESEARCH BUILDING
HONG KONG, 2005

"It was not until around 2005 that we were successful in bringing vegetation continuously up the building. This is the Genome Research Building at the University of Hong Kong, and you can see that what I did was to have a special weaving planter box at the side of the building that brings the vegetation from the forested area at the back of the site all the way up to the top of the building. The continuous vegetation idea was successfully implemented here, but I wanted to extend this idea to all the façades."

"Architecture as our built environment has to integrate with the natural environment. It is unsuccessful biointegration that has led to much existing environmental impairment and to issues such as global climate change."

KEN YEANG

<u>SOLARIS SCIENCE CENTER</u>
SINGAPORE, 2010

The Solaris is a fifteen-story office building located in Singapore's one-north business park, a hub for the research and development of media technology. The core of the Solaris building is its central atrium, within which the office floors are connected by bridges. A 1.5 kilometer-long ramp penetrates the façade and spirals up to the top of the building. A series of roof gardens connect to the nearby park. With over 8,000 square meters the building achieves more green space than the site's existing green area.

"Added to this spiraling vegetated ramp is a walkway, located next to it so that people can walk and service the planters. These ramps also become a 'Vertical Linear Park' for the building, as I wanted to create a 'park-in-the-sky.' This Vertical Linear Park's walkway, when it hits the corner of the building, opens out into a terraced area. This is probably the longest Linear Park in the world."

Framework for Ecodesign
green design as biointegration

Symposium 2016

Alina Schick
Daniel Roehr
Gerhild Bornemann
Azzurra Muzzonigro
Marion Waller
Klaus K. Loenhart
Christoph Ingenhoven
Richard Hassell
Wong Mun Summm

THE GRAVITY OF PLANTS

The biologist and agricultural scientist ALINA SCHICK has been working on the alteration of gravity sensing in plants since 2009. Based on her research, she developed a prototype which allows small trees to grow horizontally by suspending them at a ninety-degree angle and rotating their longitudinal axis.

With her start-up VISIOVERDIS she is developing innovative products that are a combination of technology and botany to solve current problems in megacities.

Products like the GraviPlant allow plants to conquer new living spaces, and allow multi-layered greening of façades. This allows severely increased biomass on vertical areas, leading to a better microclimate, increased air filtration, fixation of CO^2, production of O^2, noise reduction, and more. The agricultural background leads to an expansion into the field of vertical farming.

ALINA SCHICK: "The whole story started with my personal interest in gravity and plants. I studied biology with a focus on gravitational biology. I worked with gravity sensing in plants and I was even able to do a parabolic flight in order to sense microgravity myself.

We started to rotate cherry trees, apple trees, and plum trees, and we quickly noticed that the plants still grew just fine in our laboratory in Hohenheim. Our prototype at the University in Hohenheim (previous page) has been turning for two and a half years. Now, we've developed a high-tech plant care system which allows us to green façades in a very new approach. By rotating plants continuously on their axis horizontally, they sense gravity and light in a different way and therefore grow horizontally. In this way, we can green façades up to 2 meters in front of the cladding. That means that, in combination with available façade-greening elements on the market, which are normally very close to the façade, we can really increase the biomass of the building a lot. The GraviPlant also has an integrated long-term care system, with a watering tank and sensors in the soil which measure soil humidity or temperature. With this system, we can take care of the specific needs of many different plants."

"We green facades up to 2 meters in front of the cladding and combine our system with other wall-greening systems. By doing this, we can enhance biodiversity to a range previously unimaginable." ALINA SCHICK

1

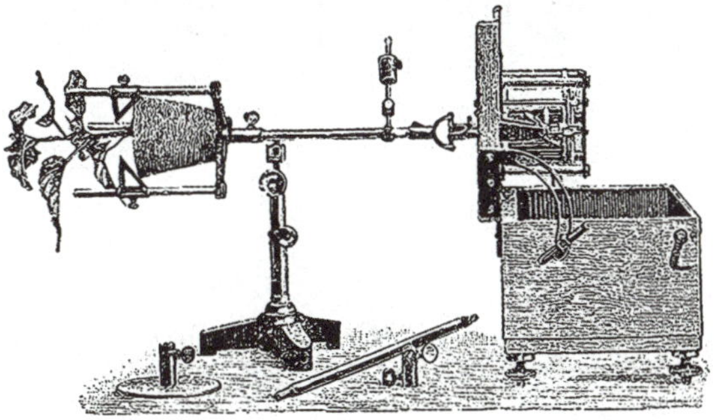

2

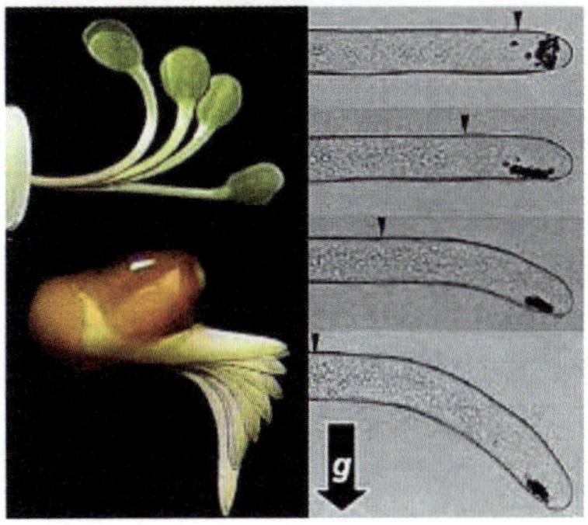

3

1 Alina Schick in her laboratory
2 *Clinostat*, Julius von Sachs, 1879 **3** The gravity sense of plants

URBAN WATER MANAGEMENT

In addition to the positive effects of plants and their planting medium in an urban environment, DANIEL ROEHR sees them as tools to manage storm and rainwater due to their high evapotranspiration rate. Daniel is founder of GREENSKINSLAB, and teaches Landscape Architecture at the University of British Columbia researching storm water management with vegetation.

DANIEL ROEHR: "Increasing impervious surfaces in urban areas, in conjunction with climate change, had a huge impact on creating recent flash floods.

A green roof is an engineered system, and it is important to understand the plants and their growing conditions in relation to the climate. There is a huge network of people designing living roof assemblies now. These processes are very complex and require interdisciplinary communication and a common knowledge base at the planning and construction stages, and especially continuously after completion at the facility (maintenance) table.

Architecture and plant material are combined into a holistic system. Vegetation is used as a tool to manage and mitigate stormwater, and recycle and reduce it on site."

"I see plants and their growing medium as tools for stormwater management and mitigation."

DANIEL ROEHR

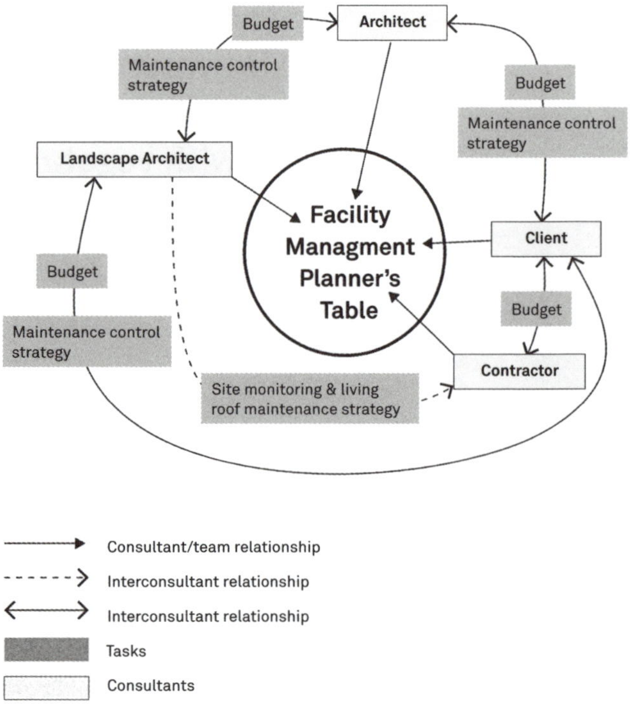

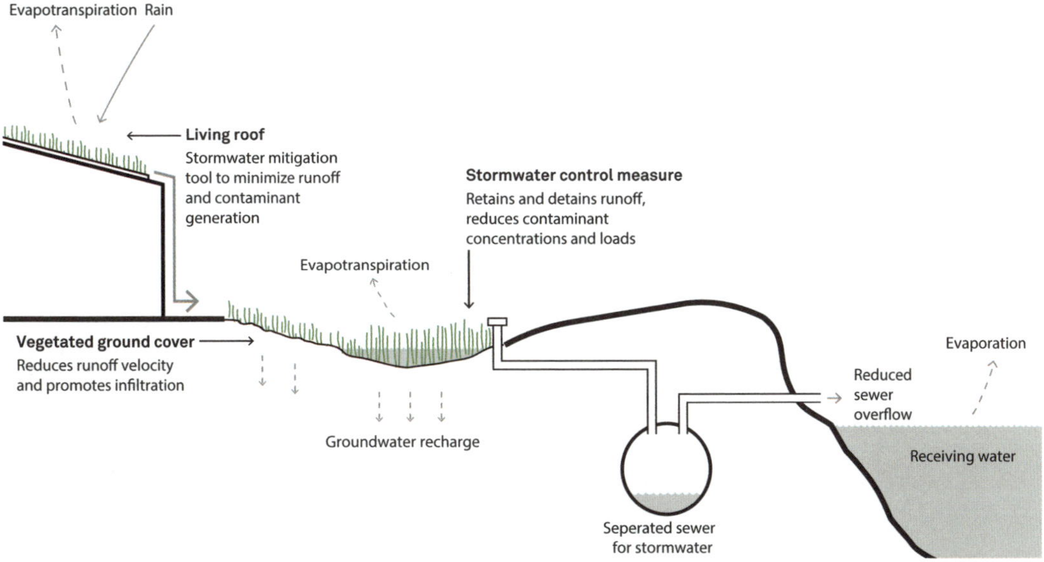

Living Roofs In Integrated Urban Water Systems

CLOSED-CYCLE FOOD PRODUCTION

Cities could benefit from the biological recycling systems and on-site food production facilities designed for space stations. The ecologist GERHILD BORNEMANN works on closed biological systems for space applications as well as their application in future agricultural systems.

GERHILD BORNEMANN: "Closed habitats like the ISS or Neumayer Station are far away from supply points, resulting in such long traveling times that the supply of things like food is very costly.

We developed a system called C.R.O.P.®, which is short for Combined Regenerative Organic Food Production. The system involves filter tubes filled with pumice, which is a very porous material. The filter tubes are equipped with a tank filled with urine and a pump that continuously circulates the urine through the filter.

The pumice is a habitat—it is an ecosystem. We inoculated it with bacteria and microorganisms from the soil to transfer the soil's functionality into space. The microorganisms and bacteria in the filter biologically degrade the urine into inorganic compounds which are suitable for plant nutrition, thus providing the link between consumption and resupply of food. We are very proud of our low-tech approach because everyone can handle such a system—you just have to maintain the pump and make sure that the filter doesn't clog.

The nutrient solution produced by the filters can be used for plant cultivation in modern hydroponic or aeroponic systems. One of the laboratories in which the C.R.O.P.® solution is tested is the EDEN Laboratory at the DLR Institute of Space Systems in Bremen. Our colleagues there are concerned with the integration of greenhouse technologies with the objective of maximizing the output per unit area."

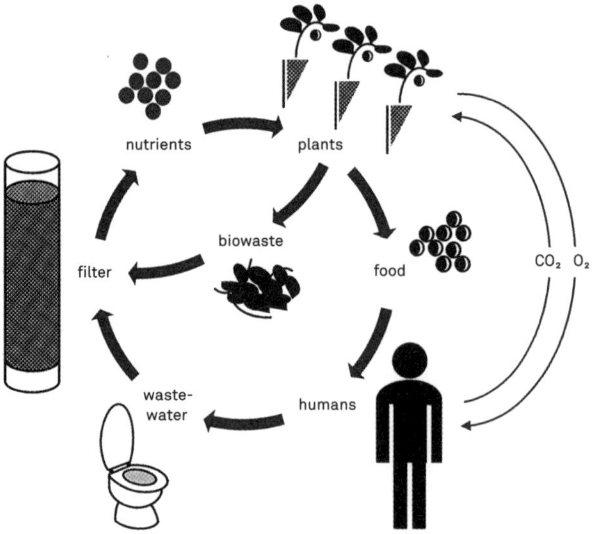

1

2

3

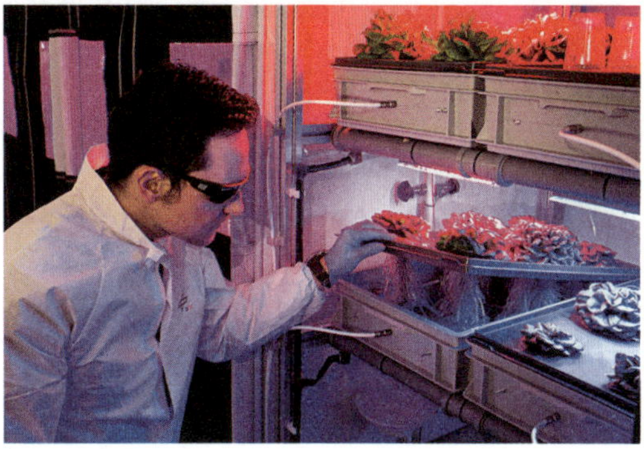

4

1 International Space Station **2** Neumayer Station **3** C.R.O.P.® **4** EDEN Laboratory

> **"We need closed habitats to live in space. We already have the ISS and want to build stations on the moon and on Mars. For these stations we need biological recycling systems, because we have to produce food on the spot. These closed environments are highly artificial. It is an advantage to have plants that are able to give humans the good feeling of being at home in space. Of course, this is similar to life in a big city."**

GERHILD BORNEMANN

"The satellite Eu:CROPIS (Euglena and C.R.O.P.® In Space) is a DLR project in cooperation with several scientific and industrial partners. The satellite is a test bed for the function of the C.R.O.P.® recycling system under lunar and Martian gravity. Accordingly, it contains a miniaturized filter and greenhouse. The gravity conditions on moon and Mars are simulated by rotation of the cylindrical body at the corresponding speeds.

When the satellite reaches its orbit and rotates at correct speed,urine is added to the filter to produce fertilizer. The fertilizer is led to the greenhouse where the tomatoes will start growing. In the initial phase the plants do not produce oxygen, but need oxygen to germinate. The microorganisms in the filter also need oxygen for the degradation process. That is the reason for the presence of the Euglena culture in the system. Euglena is a unicellular algae. When it receives light, it is activated and starts producing the oxygen needed by the rest of the system in the initial phase.

These closed-loops and low-tech approaches allow for more sustainable food production. For example, when they are integrated into the urban infrastructure, we would have local production, local waste treatment, and local wastewater reuse, as well as all the positive effects of plants in cities."

1

2

3

4

"Of course, when we do research on closed habitats we also think about what we call 'Terrestrial Applications'—what we can do on Earth with our systems, and not only in space."

GERHILD BORNEMANN

1 + 2 EDEN ISS Container **3** System MPM Test Eu:CROPIS **4** Engineering concept of a plant growth module, NASA

GREEN RIVER MILANO

Green is not just a matter of aesthetics for AZZURRA MUZZONIGRO. It is the basis for creating ecosystems that trigger cycles of life. As research coordinator for STEFANO BOERI ARCHITETTI, Muzzonigro has been working on the project Green River Milano which proposes the transformation of the old railway network in Milan into a series of connected parks. Highrise buildings ensure that the public space can be financed and used by the citizens of Milan.

GREEN RIVER
MILANO, 2017–

The Green River Milano project proposes the transformation of the old railway system into a series of connected parks. High-density buildings at the perimeter of every old train station plot ensure public and collective use as well as the financing of each site.

AZZURRA MUZZONIGRO: "One of the biggest challenges in Milan today is that there is a whole ring of railways. This railway system is abandoned and disused. The whole ring of the railway system is owned by just one public owner, which is the railway company. That is the good news, because due to this fact there is only one contact person.

The situation provides an opportunity to create a unitary urban system—the so-called 'Green River'—as a continuous green corridor. We propose to enlarge the surface and bring the unbuilt spaces to at least 80% by pushing the built volumes to the edges. The main goal is to create compact and unfragmented green spaces that are permeable at street level.

These 'Green Lakes' will be connected by the railway system and should act as an ecological corridor."

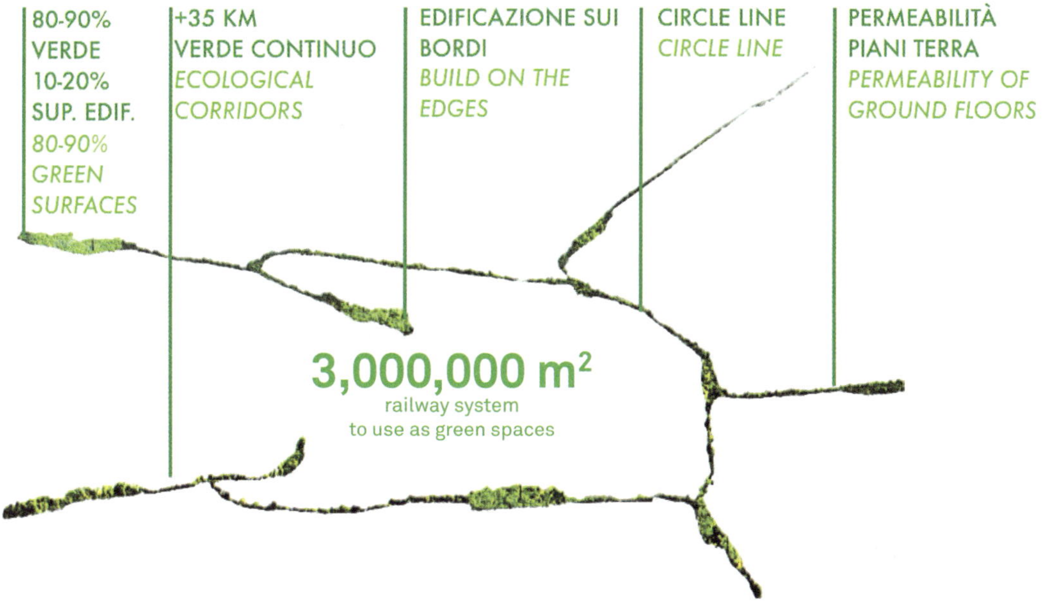

"We shouldn't use green just because of its aesthetics. We should create a green environment that creates eco-systems that trigger cycles of life."

AZZURRA MUZZONIGRO

REINVENTING PARIS

Working as the ADVISOR TO THE DEPUTY MAYOR OF PARIS for Urban Planning, Architecture, Attractiveness and the Greater Paris Projects, MARION WALLER is searching for ways to green up the city. Recently, she has been the lead advisor on the competition reinventer.paris, an international call for innovative urban projects on twenty-three Parisian sites.

MARION WALLER: "Why should we reinvent Paris? Paris is loved for its museums, for the Eiffel Tower, and for its history. People think Paris is great, so why should it be reinvented? The problem is that people have an image of Paris that is usually based on its past. But Paris is also a metropolis of the future. How can the city of Paris encourage architects, developers and other people to develop innovations?

It is important to understand that Paris is a very small and very dense city. Available land in Paris is always wasteland in very complex situations. As a consequence, you have to be even more innovative than anywhere else. The reinventer.paris competition was launched two years ago in 2014 to foster more innovation in the city of Paris and to promote more green spaces in future projects.

The idea was to change the rules of the game, because in any city today you are confronted with the same actors, the same real estate developers, who aren't innovative because they don't have the incentives to be innovative, and they are especially not innovative at all in the field of greening buildings.

Twenty-three very different sites owned by the city of Paris were chosen. The competition asked for the most innovative proposals developed by interdisciplinary teams consisting of architects, real estate developers and, most importantly, the final users.

The competition was a great success. 372 projects were submitted. For some sites, there were up to forty-seven submissions from all over the world.

In the competition brief for reinventer.paris, we asked for projects to enhance biodiversity and promote nature in the city, initiate energy transition, and improve the quality of life."

1

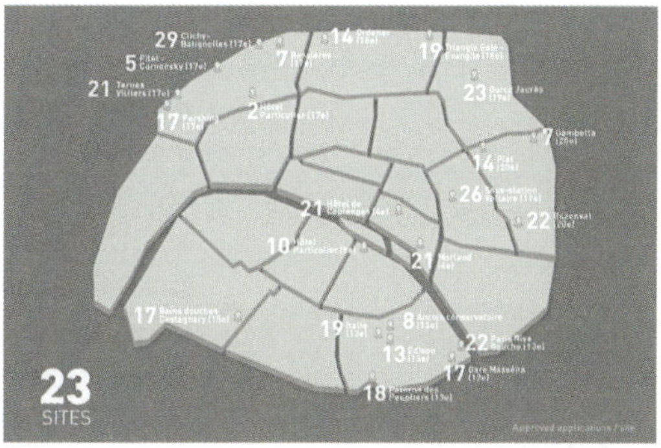

2

3

1 *Vue panoramique de l'exposition universelle*, 1900 **2** *23 Sites in Paris* **3** reinventer.paris competition

MILLE ABRES
PARIS, FRANCE

"This site is located in a very special urban situation—a space over the ring road. That means that the city of Paris was basically selling air. The winning project, which was the best financial offer, but also the most innovative concept, is called Mille Arbres, or Thousand Trees. It's a project by a Japanese and a French architect—Sou Fujimoto and OXO. It's literally a thousand trees that will be built on top of the ring road. There are two forests. One at the level of the street, which is public, and the other forest will be private. In the building there are offices, retail spaces and housing units—little houses on the top of the building. The project solves one of the major urban challenges in Paris, as it provides a link to the suburbs. And it is an idea that should be realized: it should be implemented by 2022."

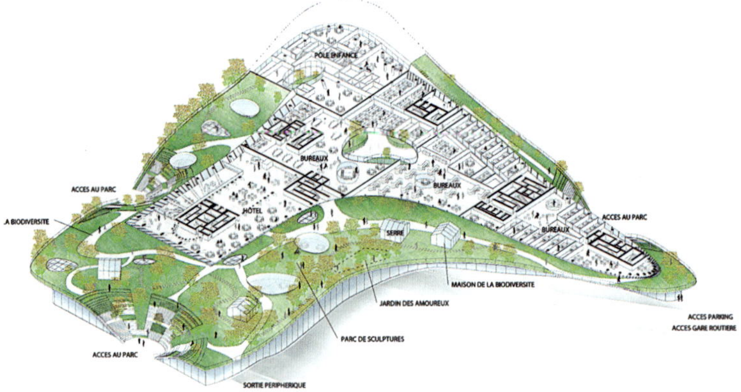

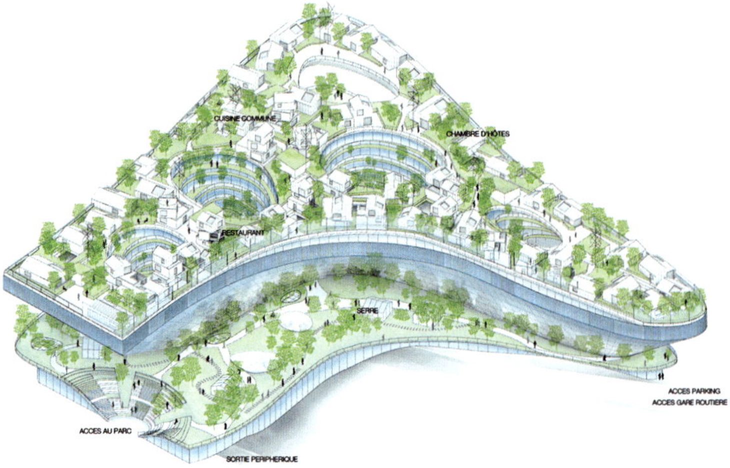

CONCORDE

1

2

3

4

"One of the twenty-three sites is a former railway station that was disused for many years, and the city of Paris had no idea what to do with it. One of the winning projects that integrated nature was Réalimenter Masséna designed by Architect Lina Ghotmeh, previously co-founder of DGT-Architects and founder of Lina Ghotmeh – Architecture in Paris. She developed the entire program around sustainable feeding, with users of the building chosen to create an interconnected ecological ecosystem. The spaces include an agricultural area set on the roof of the renovated station adjacent to the site and operated by Sous les Fraises, a sustainable food market, 'Food Culture' learning spaces for children, and an Agriculture Research Area operated by AgroParisTech, one of the major schools of agronomy in Paris.

Another project is three different buildings by XTU Architectes. They are all, of course, related to nature, but in a different way. There is a building with trees, one with plants, and this one which is called the Algo House. It will be a productive building with microalgae in the façade. Actually that's why it's green, and microalgae will be cultivated and taken from the façade for different scientific and commercial uses. The façade will be completely evolutive based on the microalgae. This is quite a risky project. We don't know how it will look like in the end, but we're interested to see what it will be.

In a city like Paris, which is very attractive, you can ask a lot of things. The problem, I think, is that a lot of mayors don't ask. When you ask developers, most of the time they will find a way to answer, because they really want to build in the cities. If you say all the buildings have to be conceptualized with a special relation to nature, they will do it. That's what I discovered with this competition.

5

6

This more historical site is an old administrative building for the surrounding prefecture of Paris—a very serious and important building. The winning project respects the existing patrimony and transforms it smoothly. It was imagined by the architect David Chipperfield and the artist Olafur Eliasson. There will be an installation on top of the building, which will be public. Up until now, it has been an administrative building, and no Parisian could go there even though the view is beautiful. When it becomes a private building, it will actually be much more open to the public, which is quite interesting. The top floor will be the work of art by Olafur Eliasson, with a special relation to the sky. Here, the old roofs of the side buildings will become urban agriculture, and it's quite a big surface. So, it's quite simple here to show that without completely transforming the building, you can have a simple intervention on an historical site, which will allow agriculture for the people living here in this building in the center of Paris."

"Until now, most architectural projects that we looked at didn't really include the questions of Hortitecture. Now the movement is beginning. We tried to find ways to green up the cities with a new political strategy; to create green spaces at all levels of buildings." MARION WALLER

1 Gare Masséna **2** Réalimenter Masséna, Lina Ghotmeh – Architecture **3** In Vivo – Tree House, XTU Architectes **4** In Vivo – Algo House, XTU Architectes **5** Morland **6** Morland Mixité Capitale, David Chipperfield Architects

RESPIRA & GODITI
IL PADIGLIONE AUSTRIA

LIVING CLIMATE MACHINE

To move beyond planting within architectural designs being just visually appealing, the key for KLAUS K. LOENHART is to incorporate a sensual relationship and what he calls "the performance of the aliveness of plants." Therefore the trained architect and landscape architect is working on bridging architectural and plant performance. With his office TERRAIN: and his TEAM.BREATHE. AUSTRIA he realized the project Breathe.Austria, the Austrian pavilion at the Milan Expo 2015. With this key project, he put a focus on the potential of vegetation to condition sensual and climatic atmospheres and the sensual experience it offers.

KLAUS K. LOENHART: "For centuries we maintained the illusion that we existed outside of nature, and nature outside of us, as an objective reference point for modern science. Nature was positioned as the other, as a stable reference and unlimited resource. When we mention architecture and vegetation it is 'either/or'. Vegetation is not normally thought of as architecture. Our bodily metabolism has developed an experiential exchange with our surroundings many thousand times more intimate than our reflected intellectual perception seems to suggest. Hearing, tasting, smelling, seeing, touching. This immense amount of subconscious data shows how strongly the sensory features of our atmospheric environment are experienced by our sensorial body. Life is in an existential metabolic relationship between the material flow of energy and information within our larger environment."

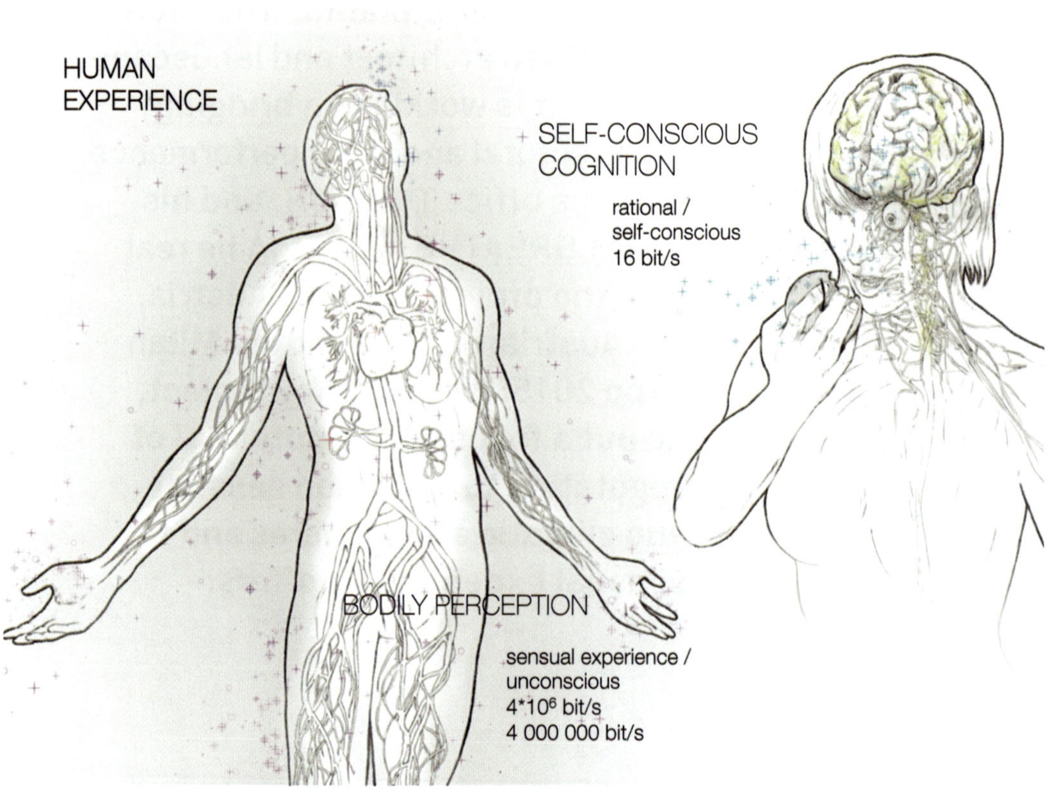

BREATHE
AUSTRIA

BREATHE.AUSTRIA
AUSTRIAN EXPO PAVILION,
MILAN, 2016

"With this ecological framing, we have set up a prototype of climatic systems for a future urban practice. The production of 'entangled things,' through metabolic circulation, then becomes a process of fusion: the making of hundreds of heterogeneous assemblages, global oxygen production, plant performance, climate conditioning, and, what is yet to be seen, the moment they all meet with social practice.

The interior landscape produces fresh air equaling as much oxygen as an average of 1303 visitors would consume per hour. We find ourselves in the living climate machine.

The natural performance of landscape metabolism becomes enhanced by the technological performance of evaporative cooling. In collaboration with Wolfgang Kessling of Transsolar a responsive fog system was developed.

The climate and the atmospheric performance has turned the pavilion into a hybrid entity where human and nonhuman performance is intrinsically entangled."

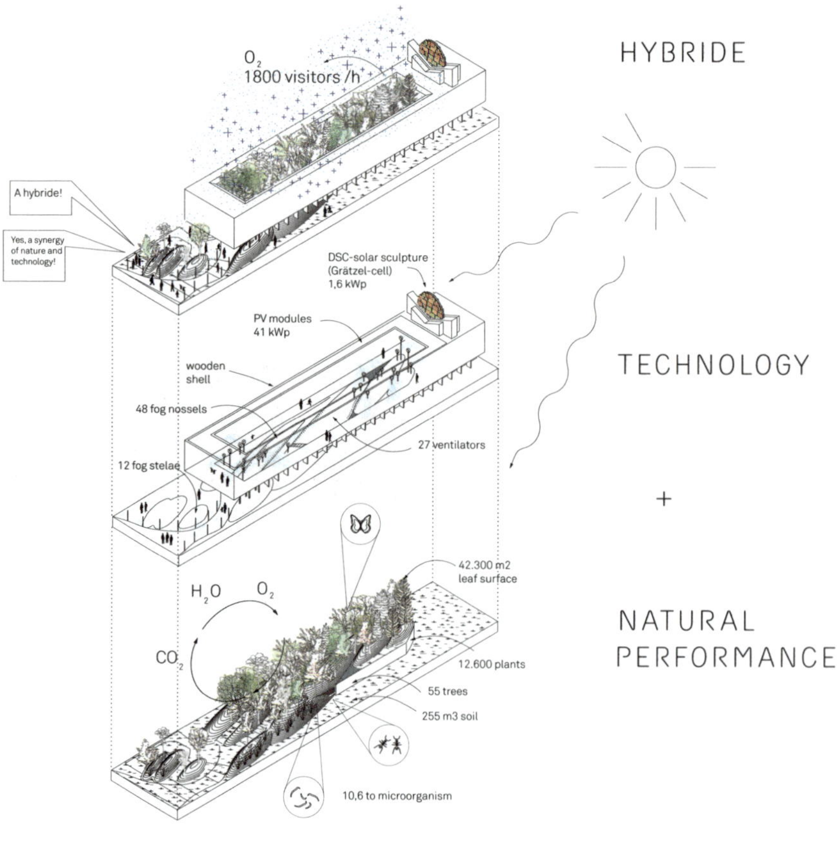

+26 °C
+26 °C
+30 °C
+25 °C
WELCOME

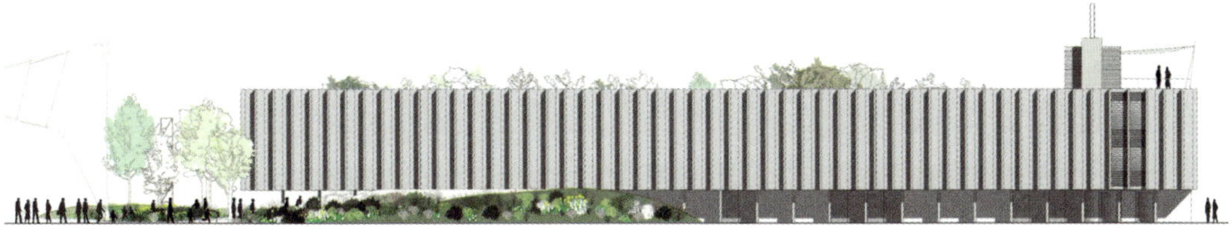

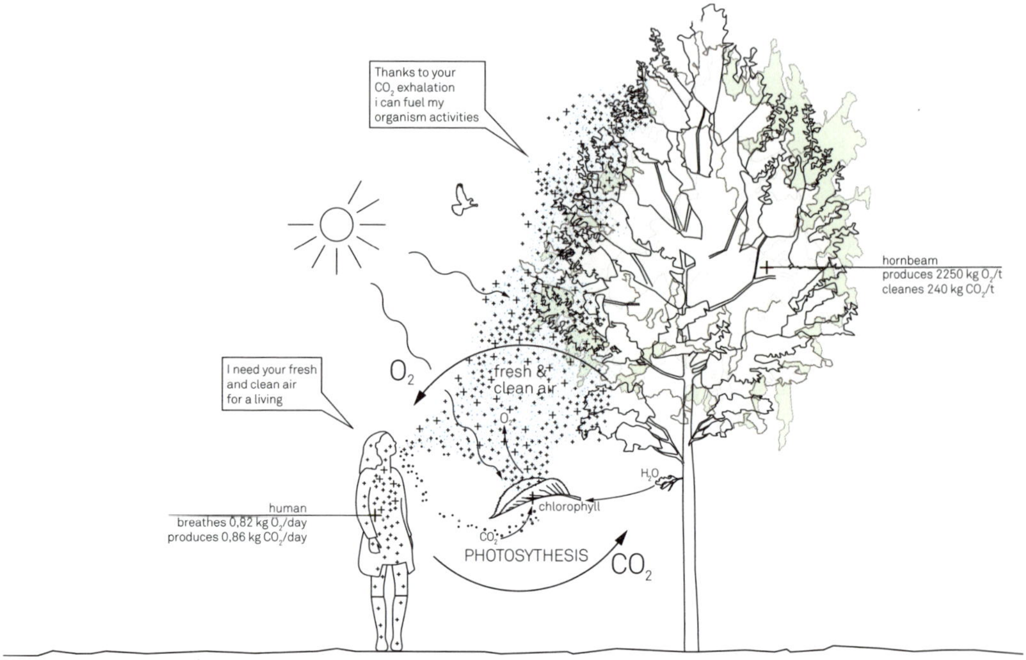

You can survive: 5 weeks without food. 5 days without water. But not even 5 minutes without air.

"Our approach is shifting fundamentally in designing with the aliveness of plants. Designing climate and microclimates through vegetation then becomes an architectural issue—approached though the interaction between the vegetative and architectural performance." KLAUS K. LOENHART

CO_2
O_2
+26 °C
sun
O_2
TRANSPIRATION
fresh air
PHOTOSYNTHESIS
CO_2
+25 °C
+31 °C
±0.00

SUPER-GREEN

The concept of supergreen®, a term shaped and patented by CHRISTOPH INGENHOVEN and his office, has decisively determined the projects they develop. It is a comprehensive concept of sustain-ability and attaches fundamental importance to energy and resource consumption in building, planning, and for the entire life of a building.

MARINA ONE
SINGAPORE, 2017

The Marina One building ensemble, made up of four towers, is located in the central business district of Marina South, Singapore, comprising offices, residential areas, and commercial areas. The façades facing the city fit into the orthogonal grid while the organically shaped interior area forms a very green public space. The office and residential complex generates more than 6,000 square meters of biodiverse parkland, connecting four skyscrapers as the green heart of the facility by implementing huge sky gardens and plants into the building.

CHRISTOPH INGENHOVEN: "The Marina One is one of the first buildings in the central business district. The general idea was to unify four plots and put this oasis in the middle. There are 3–4,000 people living in this building and there are roughly 20–30,000 people working in this building. So it's like a real city. It's a mid-sized German city. The residential tower was opened to let the air through and have turbulences. Normally we would try to avoid turbulences, but in this case we welcome them to cool the building and the courtyard. Together with Catherine Gustafson we established the idea of that central garden, and we tried, from the beginning on, to put this kind of garden not just on one floor, not just on three floors, but on nearly every floor. The oasis is a multilevel thing, and in the middle of the building we have plant rooms as well. And we have green on top of it, too. We have a waterfall there as well, which creates curtains of water. We try, in every aspect, to lower the temperature with water and plants. Two things were very important for us: one is that we give back more green mass than there would be on site if there were a jungle, and the second thing is to give back more public space to the people than the 220 meter by 220 meter building site.

We achieved 160 % public space compared to the original site area. It's not just a garden towards the street. It's really a significant part of a public plaza. And so we made sure that you can have an ongoing accessible public path through the whole building.

We bought a piece of land in Singapore, around 25,000 square meters, where we are planting all the trees that we need for the whole building. When we put them into the building, they will take some time to grow into a real garden—a real jungle."

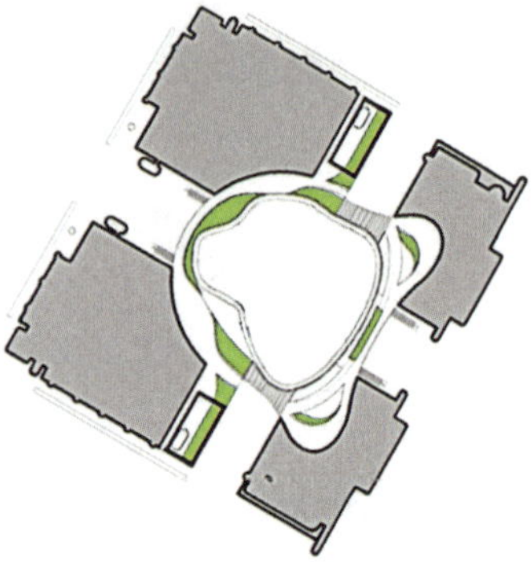

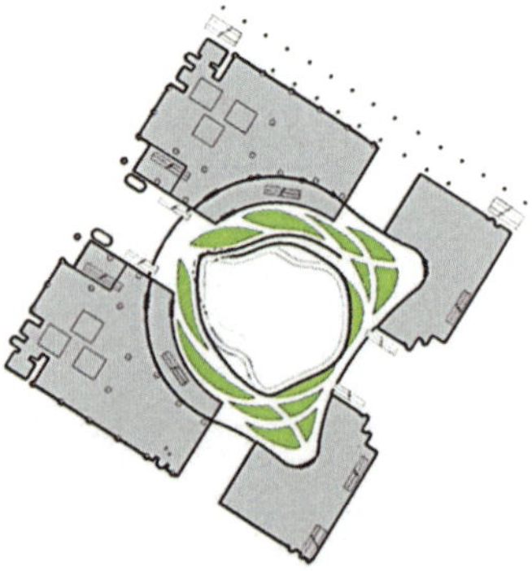

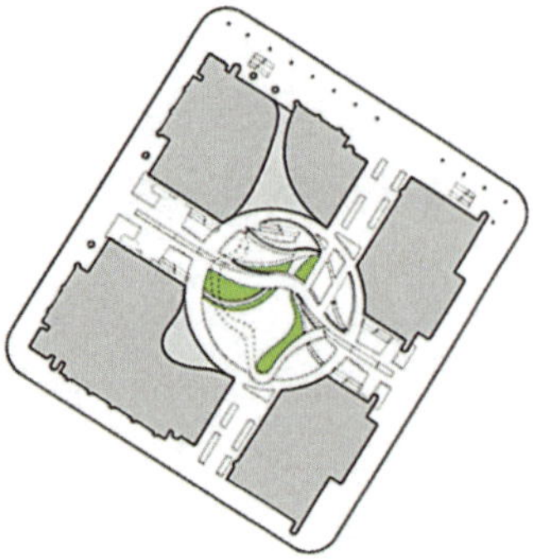

"We give back more green mass than there would be on site if there was a jungle there." CHRISTOPH INGENHOVEN

KÖBOGEN 2
DÜSSELDORF,
2014–2019

"The inner city of Düsseldorf was a very carefully designed city during the eighteenth and nineteenth centuries, and the Königsallee is the most famous street in Düsseldorf. The Second World War, and especially the time after the war, destroyed most of this street. It is a quite beautiful street, but if you look to the end of it, towards the so called Hofgarten, it looks disastrous.

So, we established the idea of building something here to get rid of all the traffic and all the misleading structures that the city built after the war. Economically, we tried to earn the money by selling land to build an underground tunnel system. So we got rid of the traffic and we also got rid of the fly-over bridges and realized that there's a beautiful ensemble of postwar architecture: the so-called Dreischeiben Hochhaus and the Schauspielhaus, a wonderful ensemble of two beautiful modernist buildings.

We tried to establish a scheme where this view between the main shopping street of Düsseldorf and these two buildings was protected by shaping new buildings. We proposed that three sides of five façades are to be completely covered by hedges. A very small building on the left side is just a kind of food court underneath, with a sloping grass lawn on top of it where people can sit and enjoy themselves. At the end of that newly created valley, you see, for the first time in history, the theater as a part of the city of Düsseldorf.

The officials wanted to have evergreen plants but I could not support the idea of integrating plants that are not native to Düsseldorf, just to make sure that they were evergreen. We checked an extensive number of different options, and one by one, had to eliminate them as toxic, deciduous, flammable, because of a lot of different problems that are caused by plants. The only one that solved all the problems was hornbeam. Hornbeam is the most normal plant you can have in Germany and I think it's the best solution, because it makes the building less special than it would have been with an exotic evergreen planting on top of it."

"It is a terraced building where you have these planter boxes which can keep the moisture in the hedge and in the plants even more. You have the general façade and then the fixings and planter boxes on top of it, and you plant the hedges into those boxes.

There are very different angles around the different irrigation systems or different kinds of maintenance accessibility, because steeper is more difficult and flatter is easier. We had a lot of structure verge into it and we have a lot of thoughts about how we should maintain it. It's a kind of agricultural industrial thing in a way, because we are planning 4,000 meters of this hedge and you have to maintain that properly.

We made a big mock-up for the 35 x 40 centimeters of soil that we have for every plant, and after one year we measured how the roots were growing and if it all worked properly. We found out that it grew well. Then we did something crazy. We had a fire test, because people were, at the end of all of this, afraid that it could catch fire. So we had to burn it. The result was nothing, I mean there was just no problem. We bought a piece of land as a nursery for this project as well and planted the hedges on it. It will be one and half years from now that we will position the plants on the building."

"Architects and landscape architects established these ideas of vertical geen walls that are really beautiful but they need a lot of maintance work. Maybe it takes a little time to get over those over-maintained green walls and get into something that is more natural. We are only in the very first phase of that kind of architecture." CHRISTOPH INGENHOVEN

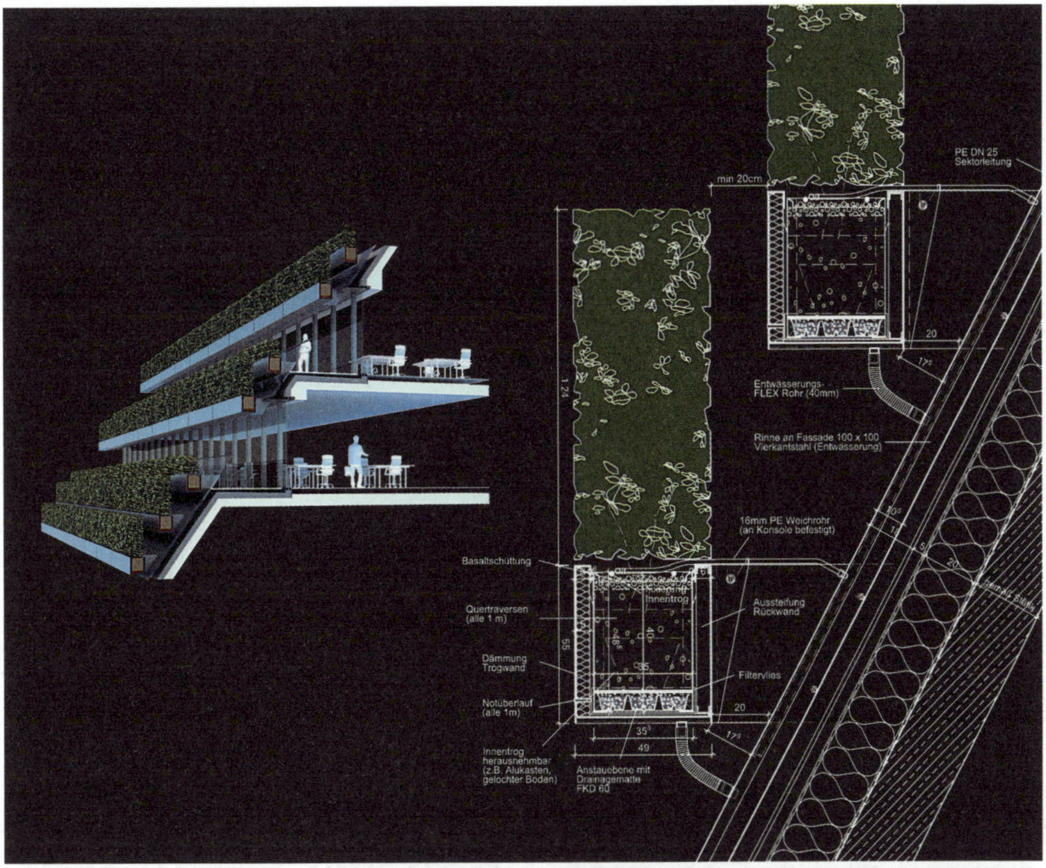
PE DN 25
Sektorleitung
min 20cm
124
20
17⁵
Entwässerungs-
FLEX Rohr (40mm)
Rinne an Fassade 100 x 100
Vierkantstahl (Entwässerung)
16mm PE Weichrohr
(an Konsole befestigt)
Basaltschüttung
Innentrog
Quertraversen
(alle 1 m)
Aussteifung
Rückwand
55
Dämmung
Trogwand
Filtervlies
Notüberlauf
(alle 1m)
20
35⁵
49
Innentrog
herausnehmbar
(z.B. Alukasten,
gelochter Boden)
Anstauebene mit
Drainagematte
FKD 60

S-a
S-e

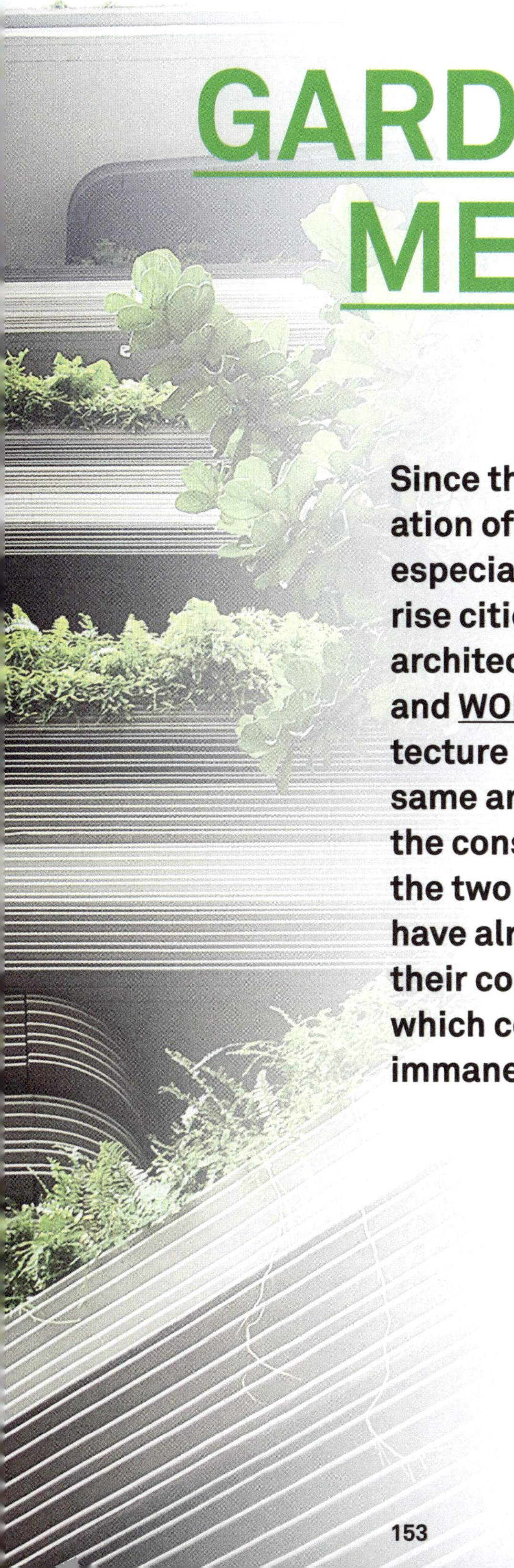

GARDEN CITY MEGA CITY

Since their main interest is the creation of more biodiversity in cities, especially in high-density and high-rise cities like Singapore, the ideal architecture for RICHARD HASSELL and WONG MUN SUMM is an architecture that enables at least the same amount of planting as before the construction. This is a claim that the two founding partners of WOHA have already implemented with their concept Garden City Mega City, which considers vegetation as an immanent part of the architecture.

RICHARD HASSELL: "There is an enormous growth of cities at the moment. When you think of these kinds of densities we really can't just roll out more square meters in twentieth-century cities. Today, we are designing one building for 20,000 people. You can't have a Garden City of the traditional nineteenth to twentieth-century density for 90 million people because it would cover the entire planet.

Macro Architecture—Micro Urbanism is a concept for thinking of the city as an enormous piece of architecture: to bring little ideas of how we navigate through the city and how we enjoy public space into very large buildings. Multiple Ground Levels, High-Density High-Amenity, Cities Within Cities, Sky Villages, Domesticated Mega-structures, and Inverted Skyline are basic principles of these future cities.

There are all kinds of performative services the plants provide, and we find it quite useful to divide them into subcategories: Screens of Green are especially green façades; Sky Gardens are public spaces or small private spaces where you can have gardens within the building; Sky Parks are something that we've been working on on several projects that join up several large buildings and connect in a continuous plan through them, so you actually get really substantive public spaces and public green spaces on top of buildings; and then Topographic Architecture is thinking of a building as a landscape, and the reason we think this is worthy of a strategy is that you have a very different relationship to an enormous building versus, for instance, a hill.

We have always tried to do extremely simple and practical green façades. One way to make them really easy to maintain is just to make sure that they are always located along circulation routes, so that the people doing the gardening do not need to have special qualifications. These are the Screens of Green at the School of the Arts in Singapore from 2005.

We realized 5,000 apartments with 1,800 private gardens for the New Cuffe Parade in Mumbai in 2010. There will be about 20,000 people living there. In 2003, we achieved 130 % of the original site in greenery through the green wall and these hanging gardens at the Newton Suites in Singapore."

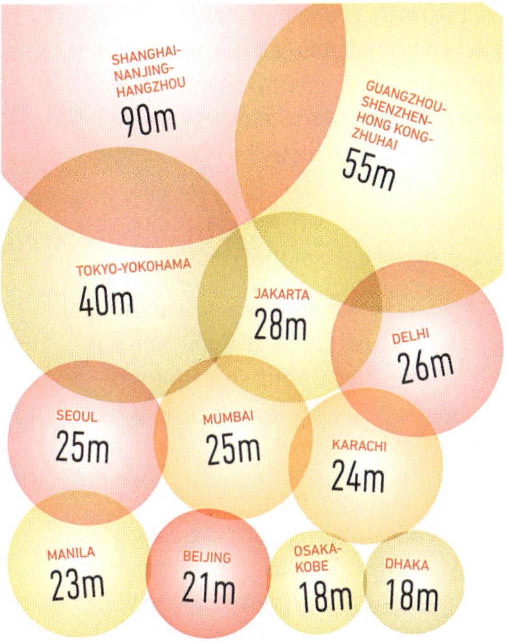

1

2

3

1 Growth of cities, WOHA
2 Golders Green, 1908
3 Macro Architecture – Micro Architecture, WOHA

"Sky Parks are one of the really interesting tools to get a High-Density High-Amenity outcome. At the Tropical Urban Business Park in Penang, Malaysia (2014), we basically looked at using the towers as pillars to support this really big park on top of the project. So here we have not only a fully open ground level with public amenities, we also have almost another ground level with private facilities and then the full public park on top of the building.

For us, Topographic Architecture means seeing a building as a kind of inhabited landscape. I think all architects are familiar with making contour models and so, in this project, we really took that idea of the topographic contours as a way of treating all the volumes in the building.

This whole area is just an aboveground car park, and normally the city doesn't allow aboveground car parks because the think they are ugly. However, underground car parks take a lot of energy and budget for a project.

When we talk to developers and city planners, I always hear about these measurements and ratios which they use to assess buildings. We are always struck by the fact that many of these ratios don't really seem to be very positive sorts of design tools. They are usually framed in a way that they are good for the developer. We felt there was a real need for other kinds of ratios to rate cities. So, the ones we felt were missing were: the Green Plot Ratio, measuring the ratio of garden to the site area; the Community Plot Ratio, which is not only gardens but public space, which shows that idea that high density will only be high amenity if we create public space in a high ratio; and the Civic Generosity Index in order to measure how the building stacks up as a kind of person in the city.

With the Ecosystem Contribution Index we can measure and rate a building and say it has Ecosystem Index of between 1 and 10. Basically 1 would be no ecosystem and 10 would be a diverse ecosystem. The Self-Sufficiency Index is the mother of all sustainability ratings and it basically compares the building to 100% self-sufficiency in power, food and water."

1 Tropical Urban Business Park, Malaysia, WOHA **2** New Cuffe Parade, India, WOHA **3** School of Arts, Singapore, WOHA **4** Newton Suites, Singapore, WOHA

1

2

3

4

"What we are really interested in is also creating more biodiversity in cities, particularly in high-density and high-rise cities like Singapore. Plants are definitely a lot more complicated than architecture because these are living things that are programmed through their DNA. They need certain conditions and you can't will them to behave the way you want. You just have to work with different plants until you find the one that's best." WONG MUN SUMM

PARKROYAL ON PICKERING
SINGAPORE, 2007

"The Parkroyal on Pickering in Singapore (2007) is really in many ways one hundred percent aesthetic. We thought, if we can find a way to deal with the car park in a positive rather than negative way, in the city, then we might be able to naturally ventilate and naturally illuminate the car park. We would have something that was so much more sustainable, and we would be able to improve the financing, because doing all this treatment on the façade was so much cheaper than the cost of excavating and the inevitable time delays on the project to create a large basement underground.

Continuing with the ideas of making it a landscape, this idea of the landscape and terraces and the mountain went all the way up the project, and we carved out all the public areas for the hotel so they feel a bit like caves or grottos."

SKYVILLE@DAWSON
SINGAPORE, 2015

The apartment house Skyville@Dawson gives the large-scale, densely built residential building the qualities of a small-scale settlement through public, external, shared spaces, which are interwoven from the ground to the roof through the cluster of towers.

"This project is a public housing project in Singapore. It is basically for the middleclass of Singapore's population. The costs were $150 million for a thousand apartements. So, it costs about $150,000 per apartment. Every apartment belongs to a cluster of eighty homes, which are gathered around these Sky Gardens to build a sense of community. This is the public park at the top of the building. You can actually jog for 400 meters around the loop with these amazing views. You see on the cross-section here, however, that these new ground levels create spaces within the building that have much more of a domestic scale. We did it in a scale so that even from the highest floor you can still recognize somebody's face and it's still within a sort of calling distance where you could call out 'hello!'"

OASIA HOTEL DOWNTOWN

SINGAPORE, 2016

The optical impression of the Oasia Hotel differs very much from the steel and glass façades of the surrounding skyscrapers. Designed as a tropical "living tower," the aluminum mesh panels in various shades of red, which in the course of time will grow twenty-one different climbing plants from the troughs behind them, form a mosaic of red and green tones. Tropical protected spaces form the upper portion of the building. Due to its special structure and design, the building reproduces 1100% of the site it occupies as greenery.

"This project is really more like an enormous garden structure. Here we managed a sort of singular achievement in that we built a Green Plot Ratio of 1100%. So, this project actually has eleven times as much garden as if we had not built a building at all.

So the building is red but it's completely planted with creepers, and so as the creepers grow it changes from red to green. We think that's a kind of interesting dance to watch across the façade as the first initial stage. And then if one plant dies you reveal the red façade again.

Some of these plants have very large purple flowers, and when the flowers drop they move like little helicopters. So the streets have these beautiful little purple helicopters floating down 200 meters onto them.

We have twenty-one different species of creepers. Although it looks more difficult to maintain, it's really easy behind the expanded mesh façade. We just have walkways and very large but quite domestic planters that the creepers grow in."

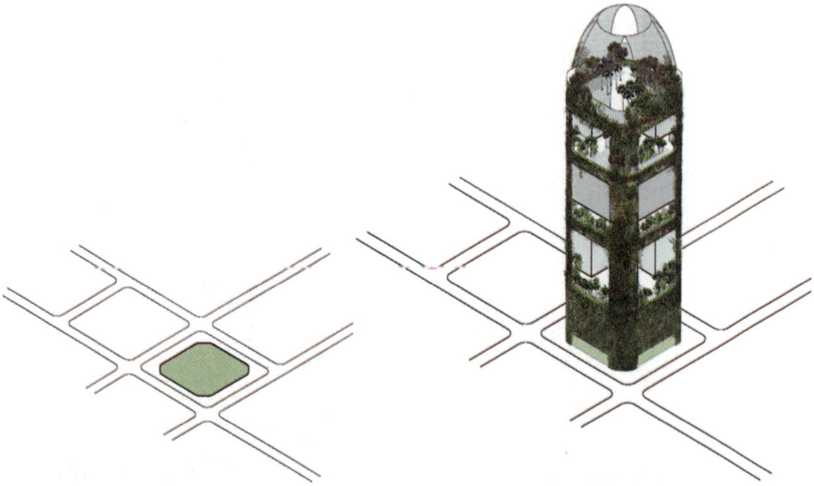

"We have the romantic vision that architecture just pushes nature up on top of it—and so you have a whole city happening, but at the same time you have as much nature and biodiversity as you had before the city was there, and we think if we can achieve that it would be an amazing place to live." RICHARD HASSELL

Symposium 2017

Gerhard Zemp
Wilfrid Middleton
Marco Schmidt
Chris Precht
Maria Auböck
Dieter Volkmann
Susanne Thomaier
Thomas Corbasson
Niklas Weisel
Diana Scherer
Elisabeth Kather

INDOOR LANDSCAPES

GERHARD ZEMP is the founding partner of APLANTIS, a company specializing in the cross-functional and transdisciplinary approach to interior as part of urban green infrastructures merging architecture, horticulture, and engineering. Key projects by Aplantis include the renovation of the sky gardens of the Commerzbank Headquarters in Frankfurt.

GERHARD ZEMP: "Gardeners often do not understand the language and underlying code of the architectural design. I think most architects are including the idea of sustainability in cities to win a competition—a lot of green in and on the building. In a standard architectural competition teams and groups of architects and landscape architects are a standard demand. My experience is that the architects and landscape architects meet at the beginning of the task. Then they work loosely next to each other on the drafts and concepts, and in the end they merge these together and the result works poorly in both the classic building and the landscape planning, but even less well in the building greenery. Both disciplines have their professional pride and feel disrespected by their counterparts.

Aplantis interacts between the architects, landscape architects, and gardeners. We often merge both aspects together and help relieve fears and prejudices. We set boundaries and define new interfaces. The result is often surprising and takes the project to a higher level, a step further. The vegetation and the building have to be planned simultaneously since they are parts of one ensemble.

Most of the planning offices, architectural offices, work from a big to a small scale. We ourselves are planning from small to big. Our starting point is the human being in the immediate work, leisure, and living environment. A lot of architects and interior designers avoid the interior green out of fear of nature. It's too wild, it's too uncontrollable. They are afraid of leaking water and unforeseen expanses. You can read about a lot of failed projects in the press. So nobody has got enough courage to experiment.

The indoor greenery is a forgotten and underestimated discipline in the discussion about green infrastructure in the dense cities. Our search for the historic roots of the building green demonstrates the importance as well as the value of earlier concepts and implementations. The heritage of our pioneers and the groundbreaking faults need to be protected and preserved for future generations. We are also engaged in renovation projects like the Commerzbank high-rise in Frankfurt, repairing old or failed green concepts."

1

2

3

4

5

6

1 + 2 Roof garden Karstadt, Berlin Hermannplatz, Philipp Schäfer ca. 1930 **3** Haus Arne Jacobsen, Hansaviertel, Berlin-Tiergarten, Arne Jacobsen 1958 **4 + 5** Haus Schminke, Löbau, Hans Scharoun 1958 **6** Congress Center, Zurich, Haefeli, Moser Steiger Architekten

COMMERZBANK
FRANKFURT, 2017

The Commerzbank Headquarters was built by Norman Foster Architects 1997. Aplantis renovated the sky gardens and developed a new planting strategy as well as detail design and construction management. These gardens in the sky are social meeting points in the village-like clusters of offices, as well as a natural climate machine to bring fresh air into the atrium—which is ventilated by the chimney effect of the vertical space.

"The building includes nine interior gardens on various levels: three gardens in the south, three gardens in the east, and three gardens in the north face, and also one outdoor garden on the top of the building.

The problem was based on the misinterpretation of the climate condition. The planting never really worked and had been replaced many times. However, we learned from the twenty years of experience of expensive and unsuccessful maintenance. We studied the gardener's failure list of plants and the success list. We were able to adapt a lot better to the existing climatic condition and managed to implement a more stable vegetation concept."

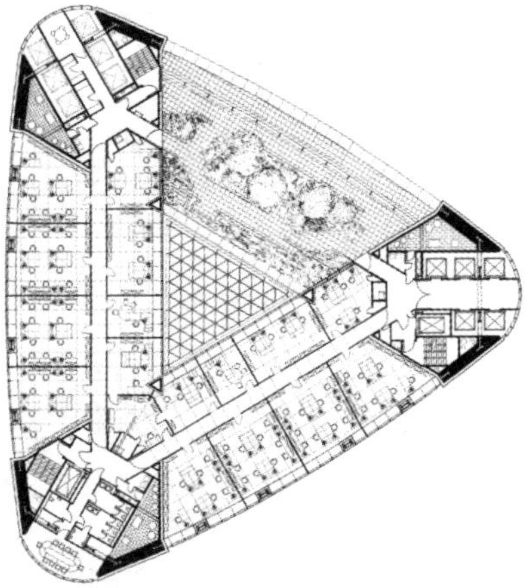

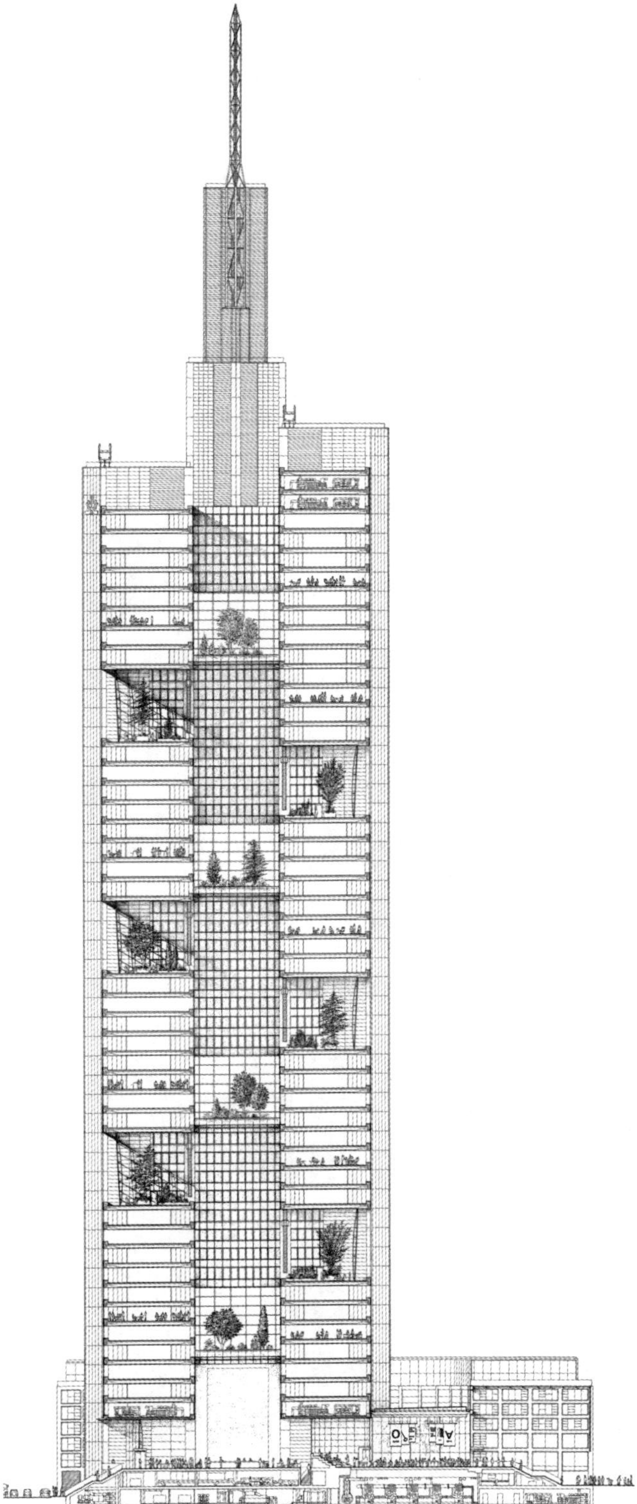

"Our role is often as a translator, a matchmaker, or a mediator, connecting horticulture and architecture."

GERHARD ZEMP

NOVARTIS CAMPUS
BASEL, 2015

Several other projects have been completed by Aplantis in collaboration with RMA Architects and Vogt Landscape Architects. One in particular is the Novartis Campus in Basel, Switzerland.

"For the Lab of the Future in Basel we greened loggias with maple trees and façades with climber plants that cover 80 % of the glazing in the summertime and 30 % in wintertime .... And we also have the indoor garden because it helps to stabilize the climate by raising the humidity in this laboratory building."

"We often work on interiors. This is the forgotten green element in the cities. The human spends 80% of the day inside buildings. Here green plays a central role. It can reduce noise and technical air humidification by humidifiying in a biological way." GERHARD ZEMP

GROWING BRIDGES

The living root bridges in Meghalaya are an impressive vernacular construction technique with living plant roots. WILFRID MIDDLETON is researching these bridges at the professorship for green technologies in landscape architecture under the guidance of Prof. Dr. Ferdinand Ludwig at the TECHNICAL UNIVERSITY MUNICH in order to make this knowledge accessible to architects and engineers and develop a new interpretation of structure for contemporary construction.

LIVING ROOT BRIDGES
MEGHALAYA, INDIA

Living root bridges are made by shaped trees. These handmade bridges are made from the aerial roots of rubber fig trees (ficus elastica) in the southern part of Meghalaya. It is a vernacular construction technique. The bridges can be up to 50 meters long.

WILFRID MIDDLETON: "There are three primary things to consider about these bridges. The first is geographic. The Khasi and Jaintia Hills are a range of hills in the south of the state of Meghalaya in North-East India. During the summer months, when the monsoon sweeps north, the clouds hit the hills and empty. It becomes the wettest place in the world.

Secondly, one must consider the Khasi and Jaintia people who live in the hills. Until recently, these constituted mainly very isolated communities with very few roads and far fewer links to the outside world than exist today. These villages constituted the same families for centuries, and this sense of continuous existence is key to the growth of such structures.

Thirdly there is ficus elastica, the Indian rubber fig. This is an amazing plant. As a strangler fig, it is a hemi-epiphytic tree, so it can grow first epiphytically on another plant, then slowly become a self-supporting structure. However, it can also grow from a planted cutting, standing alone.

The aerial roots that allow this epiphytism are a vital part of the bridge growth. The two decks of the famous bridge in Nongriat village are both grown from the tree (about 25 meters tall) on the right-hand side. The story goes that the lower deck was built first and then, when it was flooded through by the river, people thought it prudent to build a second deck.

In March, I went to these bridges and conducted some first investigations; talking to the people about the bridge histories and how they are used, measuring them to work out the sort of structural systems in quite broad terms, and then looking at specific details."

"I have been trying to get some broad ideas as to what you can do with this. So, one idea is to think about the construction process, which is obviously quite vital to understanding the bridges. Initially, one or two of these ficus trees is planted in a bank, and then a deadwood formwork is spread across the channel. The trees grow until they start to drop these aerial roots, which are wound onto the formwork and then allowed to grow further through the formwork until they find somewhere to implant or a tree to graft onto. Once they find something to hold onto they will thicken and start to produce daughter roots, and the result is a complex network of strong roots that can form a part of the pathway through the forest. The formwork is allowed to rot and then you get these bridges. This theoretically simple process is, in reality, full of complexity and variety as the bridge grows to a mature state.

First, there is a research question about these unique botanical structures and the human systems they support. And then there is the research question about solutions to modern engineering problems.

The idea of botanical structures is not new, of course. We've had treehouses for a very long time, both in the vernacular sense and the modern architectural sense. The work of Baubotanik is about taking these ideas and looking at them through a structural engineering lens and trying to work out what we can expect of these structures both in their attachments between trees and then also in attachments with artificial structures.

The bridges allow us to bring this to a larger scale. The question is how do we reproduce it?"

"We can talk about design in terms of biological and social ideas. So we should say our fundamental units of design are not the shapes we expect from the start, but the social forces and biological rules that underpin growth."

WILFRID MIDDLETON

"When we look at effective engineering solutions that the bridges provide, we might see structural optimization, which is quite a powerful learning point for structural engineering from biological systems. For instance, the University of Melbourne is doing a lot of work on bone structures to optimize the material that we use in our structures. In comparison, the living bridges appear to perhaps be very capable of resisting damage from earthquake shocks.

A lot of people are doing work on the model scale. Some models are subjected to earthquake-like force regimes and then given an iterative optimization process that is similar to mechanically stimulated changes in growth, which may be occurring in the bridges: is it possible that the bridges are adding biomass over time in different places to optimize for varied force regimes? The question is: if they do this, how? And are there things to learn?

The bridges provide a new perspective on the question of retrofitting with their natural process of decay and regrowth, which goes on throughout their lives. They grow new roots which can then be tied onto the old roots. Some bridge-builders believe that this process of decay and regrowth helps to increase the strength of the bridge over time. So in terms of retrofitting and repair this is an inbuilt system. It shouldn't be a surprise, since natural systems are full of this. For example, human skin heals itself when it gets cut.

We can look at the whole structural system and say: how does this bridge adapt for mechanical, nutrient-finding, or water-seeking stimuli? Are there particularities of the root branching or fusing that we can see are important for its structural system in creating these very complex structures? And then we can look at the individual element scale. So individual roots have shapes, changed from the circular cross section, but comparable to a lot of studies that look at subterranean roots and find that roots are optimizing for mechanical stimuli.

One of the interesting areas we are looking at are the joints. So where the roots graft onto one another, we want to know what changes structurally and in terms of vascular structure and fibril patterns."

"What can we learn about joint or material engineering, having understood that the fundamentals of design don't have to be about precise forms but more about biological rules? And we should also think about what we can learn about community integration, which is such a key part of these bridges within the Khasi Hills."

WILFRID MIDDLETON

COOLING URBAN HEAT

MARCO SCHMIDT is an expert in evaluating buildings and construction sites for storm water management, energy efficiency, and renewable energy. His work focuses on the urban heat island effect and climate change mitigation and adaptation based on evaporative cooling. He evaluates the storm water management, the green façades and the irrigation system for the Institute of Physics in Berlin-Adlershof.

MARCO SCHMIDT: "I want to explain why it is so important to green roofs and façades and improve overall energy consumption as well as mitigate climate change. The evaporation of water represents the largest energy shift at the local and global scale. The evaporation of one cubic meter of water consumes 700 kWh. It's ten times more than to heat it up from 30 to 90 degrees Celcius. If you look at an asphalt roof, for example, missing vegetation and soil shifts all the rainwater directly into sewer systems. In the summer all the incoming radiation converts into sensible heat and increased thermal radiation. This is what we call the urban heat island effect.

The environmental impact of urbanization on the water cycle is enormous. In Berlin, for instance, we receive 600 to 700 millimeters of precipitation every year. About 80% of the incoming precipitation in the catchment area is converted to evaporation. Due to the urbanization process we reduce the small water cycle of evaporation and precipitation on land more and more. And that's the reason why we dry out worldwide. If you look at all old urban developments which were founded a few thousand years ago you will find desert nowadays. But of course these cultures were not founded in a desert. The landscape of origin was tropical rainforest. Man-made land use change started with deforestation and consequently reduction in evaporation and precipitation. A heat island effect is one of the reasons why even the clouds from the large water cycle (between ocean and land) bypass and avoid rainfall.

There is a certain correlation to be identified with the global temperature and the carbon in the atmosphere over the past 250,000 years. Looking at measurements of CO^2 in the atmosphere you see a) a continuous increase from 320 to 400 ppm (parts per million) and b) an annual cycle. The annual cycle is related to the global change in the photosynthesis process; this is generally accepted. But the increase is identified as an effect of carbon (CO^2) emissions. This is a misinterpretation. On the global scale we decrease the photosynthesis process by loosing 800 square kilometers of vegetation a day.

We argue that global warming due to carbon emissions is causing drought. In my view, because we are causing drought (by deforestation and urbanization), we get climate change. We mix cause and effect in the discussion on global warming."

Dramatic Reduction in Evapotranspiration on Land
Daily Loss of 800 km² of Vegetation Worldwide

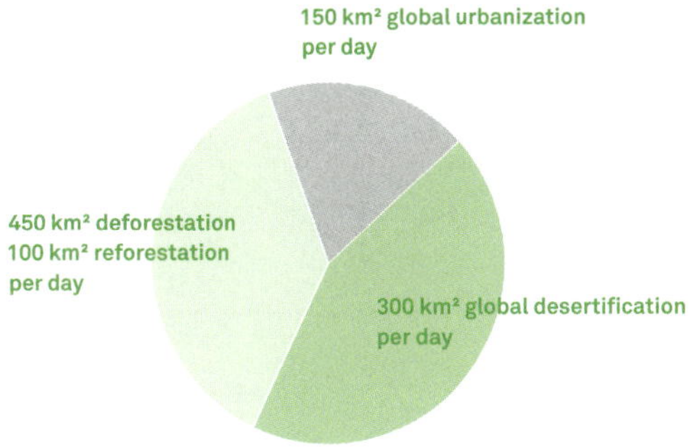

Global Radiation Budget

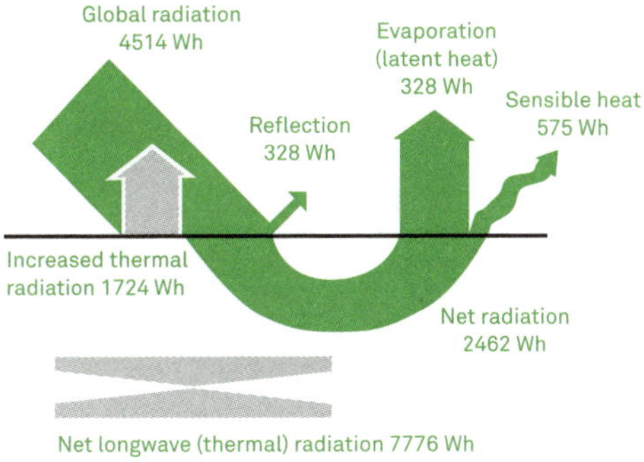

City (Bitumen roof)

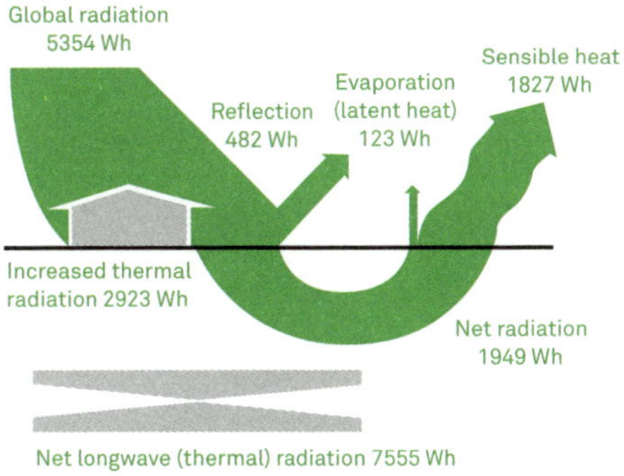

City (Green roof)

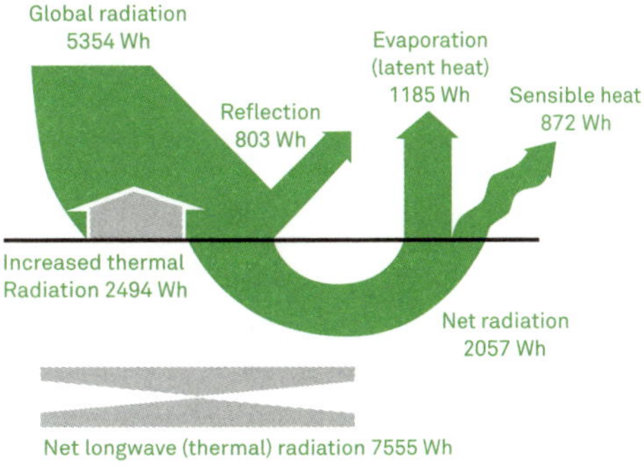

Energy Consumption in Relation to Radiation

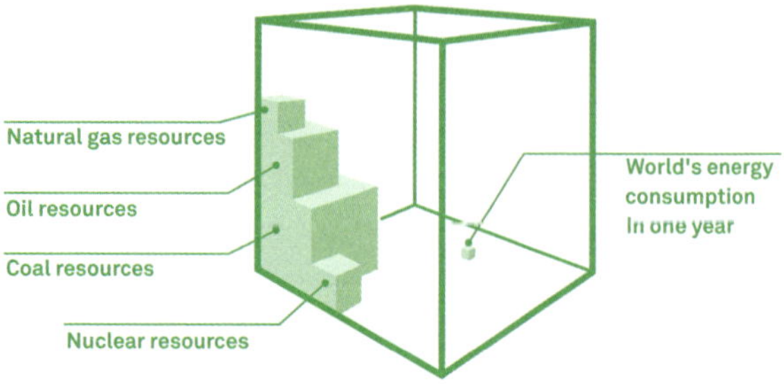

Annual Evaporation in Relation to Radiation

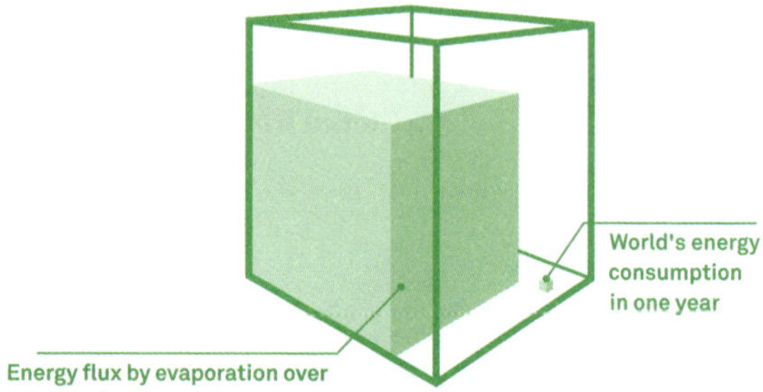

"What we need to avoid worldwide is using normal air conditioners in buildings for cooling. Instead of producing cold they produce additional exhaust heat. If you consume electricity to pump out 680kWh of energy, you produce exhaust heat of 990 kWh in the streets. This is worsening the urban heat island effect. Never use electricity to cool a building, always evaporate water instead! It's the evaporation that is missing in urban areas."

INSTITUTE OF PHYSICS

BERLIN, GERMANY, 2003

The building of the Institute of Physics Berlin-Adlershof was desigend by Augustin and Frank Architects. Due to high heat loads arising from laboratory operation and more than 70% of glass frontage, an innovative shading and cooling concept was developed and implemented: the rain water accumulating on the site is used to irrigate a large-scale façade greening. The planting provides shading and thermal protection in the summer and allows for passive use of solar energy in the winter. The construction is a mixed construction of steel and bamboo, in which floor-to-ceiling planter systems of fiber cement are suspended. The troughs are supplied by a non-conventional irrigation system. The shading and plant installation, which is clearly visible in front of the façade surfaces, is equipped with measuring equipment and scientifically tested and supported with regard to long-term energy efficiency and insights for future construction practice.

"Here we grow 450 climbing plants in 150 planter boxes and in the natural ground. They provide shade in the summer and in the winter the plants lose their leaves so the radiation passes through the glass front of the building. Conventional sun-protection systems don't evaporate water. So they convert all the incoming radiation into sensible heat and long wave emissions. With the plants, we avoid that attitude entirely."

"I developed this irrigation system for 150 planter boxes with a constant water level inside, so it is possible to measure the water consumption of the plants once every five minutes. A water level switch connected to a small control system opens a valve for a few seconds until the water level is settled.

The irrigation system is so sensitive that you can measure the real evapotranspiration rate of the plants day and night. I compare the non-green façades with conventional sunblinds to the greened ones, carrying out lots of measurements on air and surface temperatures, radiation, and humidity. A combination of measurements and simulations results in the overall energy benefit for the building. The green façade is not only cheaper in construction and operation compared to the conventional sunblinds, it is even better for the building. You dramatically reduce the amount of energy you need for cooling. If you compare a green façade to conventional sun blinds, it's cheaper in investment, cheaper in operation, better performance for the building, and better for the environment. A four-win strategy!

We're using rainwater as well, for evaporative cooling in the air conditioners. Water is evaporated to cool the exhaust air, for example, from 26 degrees to 16 degrees Celcius. Rainwater especially has a huge benefit because it is free of lime. The external air is cross-exchanged in a plate heat exchanger and, for example, cooled down to 18, 19 or 20 degrees Celsius without using any additional cooling equipment. Over the year, we save about 90% of the cooling amount; a backup only provides 10% to fulfil the overall cooling demand for this sensitive laboratory building."

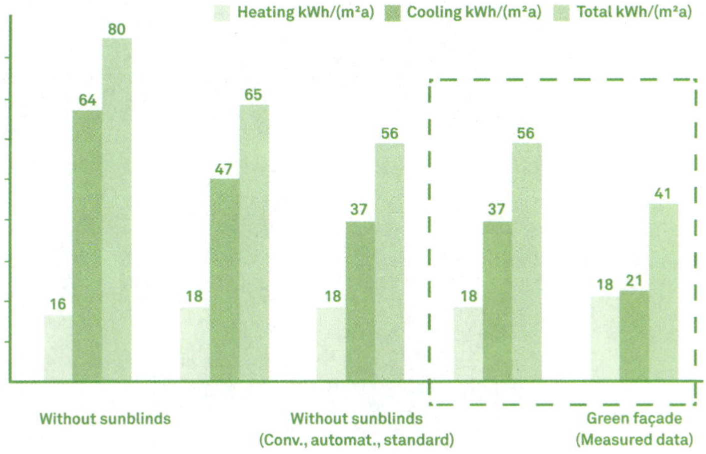

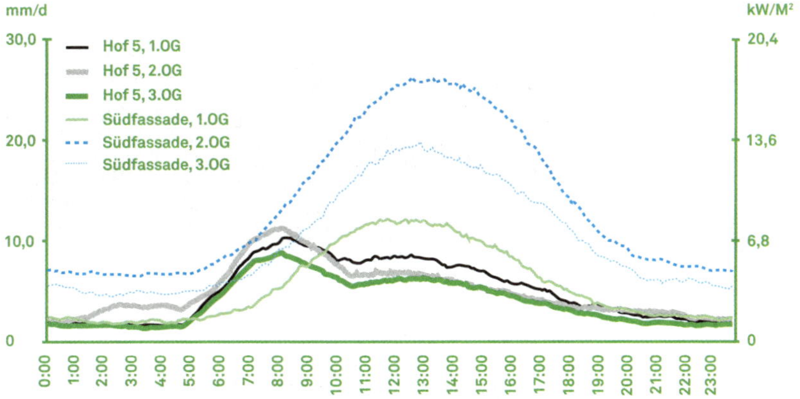

Measured Evaporation of Climbing Plants Growing in Planter Boxes

STACKING GREEN

CHRIS PRECHT, co-founder of the architecture practice PENDA STUDIO with DAYONG SUN, based in Beijing and Salzburg, sees the importance of a balanced relationship between humans and nature as a core foundation of his work. Integrating agriculture in the buildings is an essential goal of the practice in order to foster an interaction between building inhabitants and food production.

ONE WITH THE BIRDS
ASIA, 2014

CHRIS PRECHT: "Currently, we are setting up a second studio in the mountains of Austria, which is built around this idea of architecture that can bring a certain amount of vitality back into our lives and back to the cities. One aspect of this is 'vitality through natural materials.'

I was first introduced to bamboo after moving to China. The Chinese ancient building tradition is actually based on bamboo.

Bamboo has amazing capabilities when it comes to structure. It grows very fast. Some sorts of bamboo can grow up to 1.4 meters a day, and it can regrow itself from the same roots. So, when you harvest it, it regrows itself. What trees do in seventy years, bamboo does in five to seven years.

It is a great material to build with because it demands a hands-on approach, and we used it in one of our first projects called 'One With the Birds.' The project was influenced by the building traditions of the southern part of China, but also the mentality of native americans and their ancient buildings called *tepees*. Their tents are a temporary building that you can build up for the night. In the morning you can take it down again and carry it with you. This whole building process doesn't cause any harm to the material itself, nor to the site. Nature still stays natural and architecture is just a temporary occupier."

1

1 Smog in Shanghai, China **2** Bamboo weaver **3** Rising Canes, Beijing Design Week, PENDA Studio 2015

"Our focus is on vitality. We try to design buildings that have the possibility to increase quality of life. We work with natural materials, like bamboo or wood, but also develop ecological construction systems for the building process itself." CHRIS PRECHT

2

3

"Our structure is fully modular. It can extend in every direction—to the front, to the left, to the top. I grew up in the mountains, being in the wild, climbing trees, etcetera. As a kid, I experienced our natural environment in a three-dimensional way. With this approach, we try to find a way to connect people back to the verticality of our landscapes; back to the treetops.

We started with structural tests, which we financed by ourselves and built by ourselves, so that we could learn more about the capabilities of bamboo. For example, the building process, how to tie the joints, and so on. In this structure, there is no metal. Everything is tied up with ropes, and the material itself stays ecological and unharmed. That creates a temporary approach to the building and all of its parts can be reused afterwards. In its deeper sense, it's a building that can be recycled and can have an after-life. Currently we are building a surf hotel in Ayampe, Ecuador, with a four-level structure—all in bamboo.

We are starting to build a second structure in Anji, which is the world's biggest export region for bamboo. The project in Anji has a long-term approach and describes a full life-cycle. First, we are planting a bamboo grove, and for every bamboo we take out for construction, we seed two more. And this way, the natural surroundings grow at the same time as the architecture. I see that as an ecological building loop and as a sustainable alternative to the current way of construction."

"Hortitecture, for me, is a term of the future. But it is also a term which comes from the past. It means that we look at our vernacular architecture; that we look at our building traditions; that we look at traditional building materials and also how people, our ancestors, built their buildings with natural materials, and transfer all of this knowledge into a contemporary practice to reinterpret it in a modern way for the future." CHRIS PRECHT

BOTANICAL BUILDING SYSTEM
EUROPE/GLOBAL, 2015–NOW

The Botanical Building System started as a project for refugees in Europe. The aim was to develope a very flexible system that can adapt to different needs. The combination of garden and housing enables one to start their own buisness, and the modular system can grow step by step. This system can also be extended to a high-rise with private gardens and the possibility of everybody being able to produce food for themselves.

"I think that architects now also have a responsibility to think about ecological alternatives, especially when it come to our cities. My experience comes from China and in India, where I lived for five years and have a couple of projects. The cities there are growing at an enormous speed, and by 2050 I think around 70% of our population will live in urban areas.

The current way of constructing our cities is hugely unsustainable, and the building profession is using more than 50 % of all the energy on our earth. So we as architects—we are a big contributor to this pollution of our cities. So I think we really need to find an ecological alternative, to work with materials which have less of a carbon footprint and have a more ecological outreach for our cities. And I think that innovation doesn't necessarily need to be high-tech. Like, in this sense it can be also low-tech. So, to do more with less, in a way, or with something that is already known: to look at vernacular architecture of specific places and learn from them and then adapt those methods to a more modern and contemporary way of how we construct."

"Vitality through healthy architecture: this project is a modular building kit that integrates the botanical and the architectural in one design. Everything is based on an A-frame construction which is put together very quickly. Inside these triangles are living spaces and outside is space for a personal or communal garden. The project connects architecture and agriculture and hopefully both industries can benefit from it, because at the moment they are equally unsustainable.

In agriculture, we have a system in which the countryside is producing the food for everyone. But when it comes to growing food, the countryside cannot be seen in isolation anymore. The current way of agriculture emits more greenhouse gases than all forms of transport combined. It uses more than 70% of drinking water. And because we are mainly growing corn, for cow feed and syrup, the food production is a big threat to biodiversity.

We need to rethink our way of food production and the supply chain. The food-safety of our cities is one of the biggest topics of the future. Growing food in the city will be essential to feed a huge population. And the demand will be enormous. In the next fifty years, there will be more food consumed than in the last 10,000 years combined."

"And 70% of the world's population will live in urban areas, so cities need strategies on how to be involved in the production of our nutrition. And growing food in the city has a lot of benefits. The city already produces so much energy and heat. Warmth is good to grow, for example, tomatoes or potatoes. At the moment a building uses energy and blows it out the roof. We should work on solutions for how we can reuse this energy for additional things, like growing vegetables. The positive sideeffect of having plants on the façade of your buildings is that it also cools down the building at the same time, and the energy consumption of the building becomes more effective.

Food and construction are the biggest industries out there. Real food serves a community. Good architecture serves a community. Combining them can create added value to each other. I do believe that, as young architects, we need to look outside of our sector and collaborate with different industries to create an impact in a fast-changing future."

1

2

3

4

"Of course, we should have a fresh take on a modular building process in order to create variety, to create life, and to really bring buildings alive with plants." CHRIS PRECHT

1 + 2 Yin & Yang house, Germany, PENDA Studio **3** Tel Aviv Arcades, Israel, PENDA Studio **4** A Thousand Yards, Botanical Pavilion in Beijing, China, PENDA Studio

BUILDING LANDSCAPES

Keeping nature in the city is a challenge that the landscape architect MARIA AUBÖCK gladly takes up. As founder of AUBÖCK+KÁRÁSZ LANDSCAPE ARCHITECTS, she sees great potential for the next generation of architects to tackle changing climate conditions by constructing combined habitats for humans and the world of plants and animals.

MARIA AUBÖCK: "Every student understands what civil engineers do; in our view, gardeners are 'nature engineers' who know Latin. For several centuries, gardeners around the globe communicated with each other via Latin plant names. It is a cosmopolitan business. What fascinates me is that the plants, which are intelligent beings themselves, enter into a dialogue with our design. They respond to their surroundings.

In this presentation we show that it was not the Europeans who started greening buildings. An etching dating to 1725 by the baroque architect Fischer von Erlach shows the gigantic roof gardens of Babylon—which are buildings! Greening is occurring all over the world, and it's a cultural phenomenon. The cooperation between plant culture and architecture is a long-standing tradition.

Stepping back even further in history, we encounter a Persian roof garden with gentlemen sitting in the meadow. Le Corbusier's Villa Savoye roof garden is equipped with comfortable furniture and rectangular plant beds. I also found a design by the landscape designer Burle Marx of the roof garden of a bank—all of his designs inspire us. We are part of a tradition, we are part of a movement. It's a flow. And if we want to join in, we should know about our predecessors."

1 Engraving, Fischer von Erlach **2** Persian roof garden in *Spanish and Portuguese Gardens*, Rose Standish Nichols; Boston: Houghon Mifflin 1924 **3** Villa Savoye, Poissy. Le Corbusier, Pierre Jeanneret, 1928–1931 **4** Ministry of Education and Health **5** Jeanne Hachette, Ivry-sur-Seine, Paris, Jean Renaudie, Renée Gailhoustet, 1969–1975

1

2

3

4

5

JOSEPH PSCHORR HAUS
MUNICH, GERMANY, 2013

The Joseph Pschorr Haus was designed by Kuehn-Malvezzi Architects and Auböck-Kárász Landscape Architects. The inner courtyard unfolds as a terraced garden with a kaleidoscope-like glass façade that reflects and multiplies the greenery. A front elevation was designed as a three-story greenhouse that is reflected in the adjacent facades. The roof landscape on top of the fashion shops consists of a grove of Japanese maples and hydrangeas.

"The idea was to create a stepped-section courtyard garden on four levels. The shops' plant beds are situated on the courtyard roof garden, and above that there is housing, and, at the very top, solar panels and an extensive sedum landscape.

Only after having presented our design did we learn that the architects had chosen black mirrored glass for the building's outer skin. As a consequence we had to revise the whole planting project, because in August the temperature near the façade—in partial shade—reached 42 degrees Celsius. Only a few plants—for example, sage—thrive at this temperature. For the courtyard we chose lamium, a silvery plant that can withstand the heat.

In our profession, a project isn't finished once the plans have all been drawn up—we have to do supervision. Sometimes four or five years later we return to the site to teach people how to maintain and repair it."

ERSTE CAMPUS
VIENNA, AUSTRIA, 2015

Erste Campus in Vienna was designed by Henke Schreieck Architects and Auböck-Kárász Landscape Architects. The buildings include four atria with honey locusts, Japanese maples, and shrubs and ground-cover plants. The garden on the upper floor unfolds as a spacious grove of Japanese ornamental cherry trees, complemented by pines and maples.

"At the Erste Campus we had to come up with ideas for a landscape that even works with a very low substrate level.

With the architects, we developed a public site for flaneurs that linked this site to the nearby parks, to the train station, and to the city center.

For the landscape design we developed a multilayered system and integrated the structural system and the insulation layer, the gravel, the prefabricated steps, and the plants. The tree broker had to select trees compatible with a flat root system. To our surprise, in August 2017, one year after the opening, the trees planted in containers were thriving and had big leaves, while the trees planted in the ground had sparse, small leaves. It turned out that for four months the irrigation had been broken, and the facility managers had neglected to tell the gardeners."

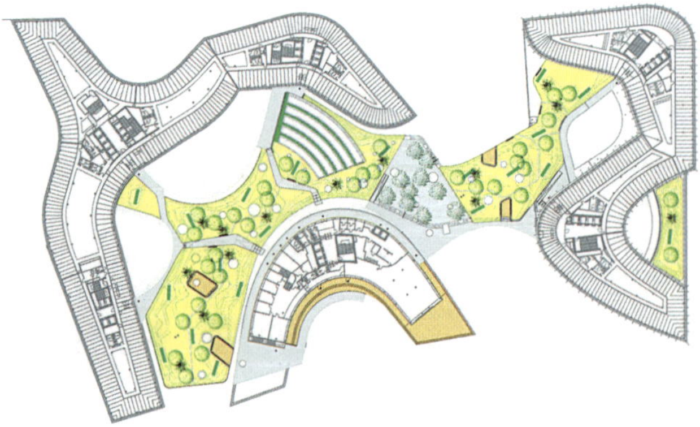

"The future aim of Hortitecture should be to think about buildings as a chance to combine plant life and human life to tackle climate change." MARIA AUBÖCK

WAGNISART
MUNICH, GERMANY, 2017

The residential estate was designed by bogevischs buero, SHAG Schindler Hable Architects GbR, bauchplan, and Auböck-Kárász Landscape Architects . The landscape architects designed a variety of collective roof gardens.

"The residential estate was implemented by the company WagnisArt. So the families who applied and wanted to be part of this joined in to discuss the urban site, where the buildings are linked by sky walks. We had twenty tenants who discussed with us the communal courtyards and roof gardens. We designed different elements for the roof—for example, solar panels and vegetable boxes. In the end, we planted all of the gardens with these residents.

You have to learn your techniques for urban landscaping! To learn what you must put in the soil to keep it fertile, to learn when you need insulation, and when you need drainage. This is really the secret to it all. We have the world of trees, the world of shrubs, the world of climbers, and the world of water plants. And we have the world of indoor greening. There are a variety of plants that you can use in and on buildings, but please work in teams and cooperate with specialist horticulturalists."

"We have to pass on our knowledge to students so the next generation will have the chance to tackle major architectural problems—including climate change. Our task is merely to prepare, correct, repair, and construct habitats. With regard to living conditions and habitats, we must come to understand what makes them sustainable—not just for people, but also for the accompanying flora and fauna." MARIA AUBÖCK

COMMUNICATION IN PLANTS

DIETER VOLKMANN specializes in communication in plants and neuronal aspects of plant life. Dieter Volkmann is an emeritus professor of the University of Bonn and started his investigation more than twenty years ago. His hypotheses that plants can taste and smell, that they even have a kind of intelligence, originally provoked a huge uproar. However, today a lot of these hypotheses have been confirmed.

The book *Communication in Plants: Neuronal Aspects of Plant Life.* was published by Frantisek Baluska, Stefano Mancuso, and Dieter Volkmann in 2006. Plants are presented as intelligent and social organisms with complex forms of communication and information processing.

DIETER VOLKMANN: "Plants are absolutely able to adapt to different situations and environments—to any environment—and so buildings are certainly one of the environmental areas which they are able to use.

Plants live in two biotopes, and this is really important because there is no other organism that does so. They live underground in a water atmosphere and aboveground in a gas atmosphere. One part of the plant is related to heterotrophy, as we are. But the other part is the autotroph part; it is the green part of the plant—the O^2 producing part. It is also the CO^2 consuming part. The lower part produces CO^2 as we do, and it needs O^2 as we need. So photosynthesis is certainly the most important process on our planet. Nevertheless, photosynthesis and root growth or root development have to be in relation to each other.

Plants are able to cooperate with different other organisms, in particular bacteria and fungi. They are able to move. They move by growth, and growth is slow. So we need time-lapse studies to see how fast plants can move. Most of the plants, most of the trees, are interconnected by fungi, and they are able to bring some nutrition and information to their neighbours."

"It is hardly an exaggeration to say that the tip of the radicle ... acts like the brain of one of the lower animals; the brain being seated within the anterior end of the body, receiving impressions from the senseorgans, and directing the several movements."

DARWIN, C.R. (1980) THE POWER OF MOVEMENTS IN PLANTS. (ASSISTED BY F. DARWIN), LONDON: JOHN MURRAY.

1

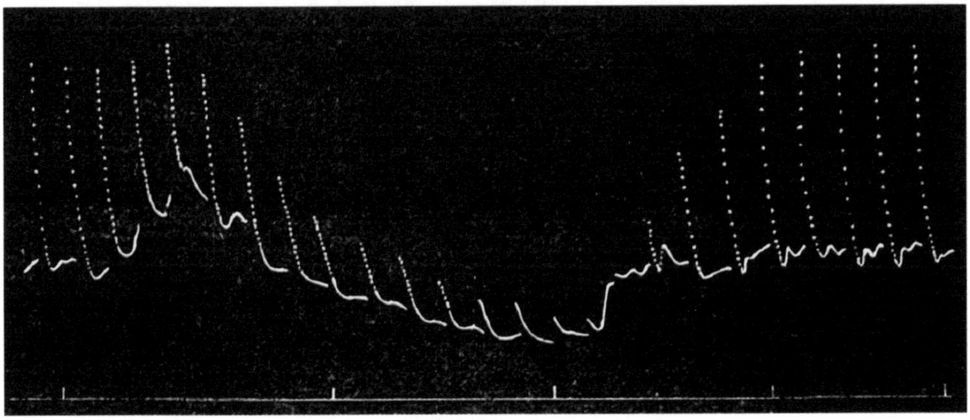

2

1 Lichtenegger et al. 1997
2 Jagadish Chandra Bose
Life movements of plants
1918/1926

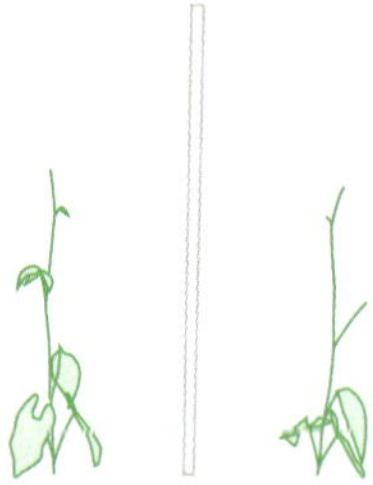

Sensing

Searching for alternatives

Giving up

Sensory System of Plants

“The diagram shows three compartments. The fungus is in the center as an ion exchanger. On the right-hand side is the soil with molecules, which are necessary for plant growth, and on the left are molecules which are transported from the fungi to the plant—already changed in the body of the fungi and then given to the plant. In the opposite way, the plant feeds sugars to the fungi. There is a well-functioning symbiosis between plants and fungi.

Plants are able to perceive orientation. The form of the plant depends on the gravity vector, which is a forming factor. Plants know that they are touched. About twenty years ago colleagues found touch genes. For vision, the plants have three photo receptors. One for photosynthesis, one for blue light, and one for red light. Plants are able to smell gases and use them as molecules for defense. Tasting is a very similar sense. It is related to the perception of solute molecules. That means if a plant is attacked by caterpillars, it is able to identify molecules in the spit of the caterpillar and to differentiate between different caterpillars, which they can also do by hearing. 250Hz is the ideal frequency.

I mentioned that there are many other performances and perception mechanisms or processes in plants. They are able to perceive electrical fields, magnetic fields, pH-value, type of molecules (mostly ions), the concentration of these molecules, and even the temperature difference. They are able to identify a neighbor, and whether is a friend or an enemy; if it belongs to their own family or if it belongs to another family. And finally, three other very important points: shadow avoidance, wound healing, and immune system. All these processes are realized in animals and humans, but in another way and in another time constant.

The upper and lower parts of a plant are working in absolutely different processes. The communication between both areas is necessary so that both can develop properly. Basis for interspecific communication is the root brain hypothesis of Darwin, the plant intelligence concept. Our idea of the decentralized coordinating system is that it is not a brain, but that it is a decentralized system—like swarm intelligence.”

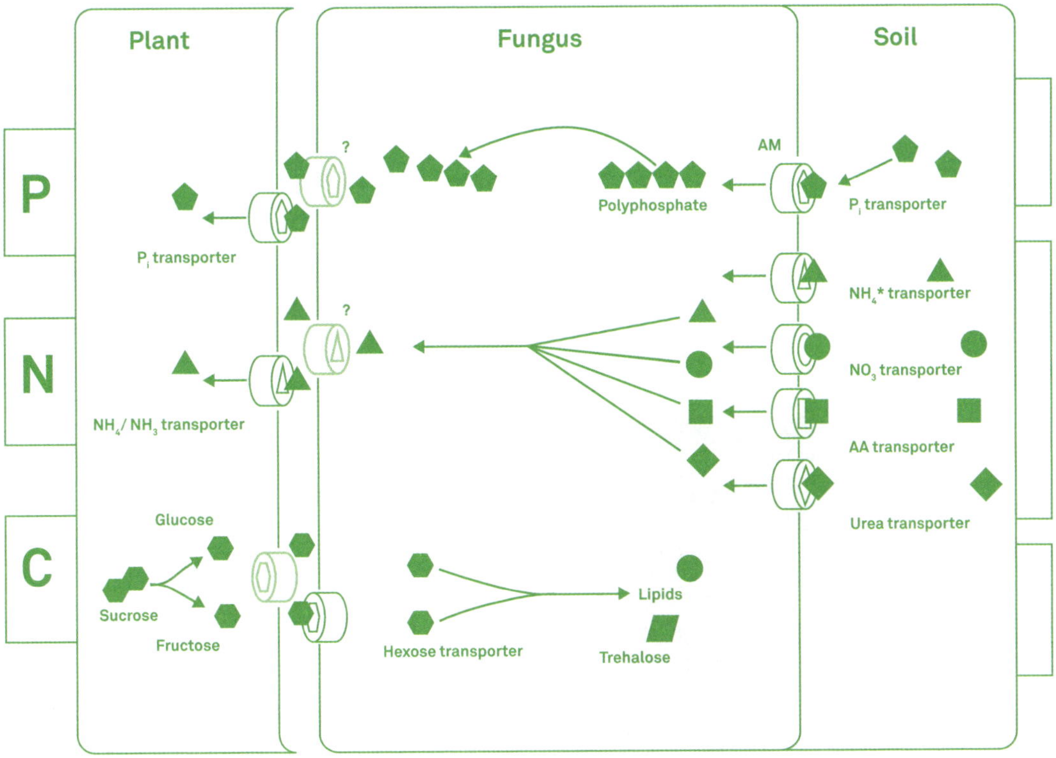

Symbiosis of Plants and Fungi

> "Plants are able to see, to hear, to smell, to perceive mechanical signals, etcetera. They need lots of signals to behave, to survive in a surrounding which they are never able to leave. These processes ask in particular for neurons, synapses, transmitters, neuronal proteins and receptors."
>
> DIETER VOLKMANN

ZERO-ACREAGE FARMING

SUSANNE THOMAIER explores the potential of farming on and in urban buildings—summarized as ZERO-ACREAGE FARMING, meaning farming without using any additional acreage. She explores and classifies the different types of current practices and evaluates their potential for a sustainable urban transformation.

SUSANNE THOMAIER: "Zero-Acreage Farming (ZFarming) is a term that we have developed within a research project and it describes the idea of growing food without using any additional land or acreage—so using the urban building stock. It relates to all forms of food production in or on buildings, encompassing enclosed environments, such as rooftop greenhouses or indoor farms, as well as open-air rooftop gardens or farms. Since the purpose and scope of ZFarming projects vary greatly, we have developed a typology describing five types of ZFarming.

The first one is commercial and refers to farming businesses: they grow to sell and make a business out of it. Instead of growing in soil, most commercial farms in or on buildings use hydroponic growing methods or aquaponic systems, where you connect the growing of the plants with fish cultivation. They are mostly working in enclosed environments such as rooftop greenhouses or indoor farms. Farms of the second ZFarming type are operated by restaurants—not necessarily for profit, but rather for image purposes. Or as the Vertical Farming Association puts it: they grow to prepare, using the produce from their own rooftop garden or indoor farm in the kitchen. So they offer the idea of 'farm-to-table' to their customers. The third type encompasses ZFarms with a social and educational focus. They are usually run by non-profit community organizations, schools, or hospitals, which grow to share, to heal, or to teach. Hell's Kitchen Farm Project is an example in New York. It is a social project on a church. They grow in small raised beds and it is managed and run by volunteers, and they distribute their produce through a local food pantry and a CSA program. And then there are ZFarms that clearly relate to urban living quality, such as open-air, soil-based rooftop gardens that serve as enjoyable amenities for the tenants of the buildings. Finally, we have also identified ZFarms that are operated by research institutions or private companies exploring and developing innovative farming technologies—mainly for indoor farming."

"We have to differentiate between whether a ZFarming project is working commercially and is operated by profitable business, or whether it serves social or educational purposes or the urban living quality." SUSANNE THOMAIER

1

2

Commercial	Grow to sell
Image	Grow to prepare
Social & Educational	Grow to share Grow to heal Grow to teach
Urban Living Quality	Grow to enjoy
Innovation Incubator	Grow to develop

ZFarming Typology

1 Hell's Kitchen Farm Project, New York City **2** Indoor farming, VertiCrop system

"Of course the city cannot support itself alone, but we can raise the part that is grown locally within the city and try to use resources in a more efficient way."

SUSANNE THOMAIER

"If we think about the potential of ZFarming in future cities, the simplest thing is to combine it with rainwater harvesting to water the plants. You could also clean and use the grey water of the building for watering the plants. Of course, the produce of a rooftop farm contributes to the food supply of the neighborhood. Besides, there are synergies concerning the heat flows of a building, since rooftop greenhouses and green roofs serve as insulating layers. Especially at times of the year when the air is still cold and the sun is shining, rooftop greenhouses heat up quickly—so that you could use the warm air from the rooftop greenhouse to heat the building. At the same time, they cool down quicker than the rest of the building, also making it possible to cool down the building with the cooler air from the greenhouse. Since CO^2 enhances the growth of the plants, the CO^2 of the building could be used in the rooftop greenhouse.

Producing food in the city also creates new opportunities for a circular economy. By connecting food production and different steps of food manufacturing within a building, waste, energy, and material loops can be closed. Waste products from one manufacturer could be utilized by another. On the other hand, there are also many challenges associated with ZFarming: they concern the suitability of the building, infrastructure, zoning and permission processes, convincing the developers and building owners, leases, acceptance on the consumer side, economic viability, pollution, and others.

ZFarming can be a great opportunity for future cities, offering benefits such as resource-efficiency, a locally embedded (food) economy, and new green spaces. The diversity of ZFarming types requires a careful assessment of the respective challenges and benefits."

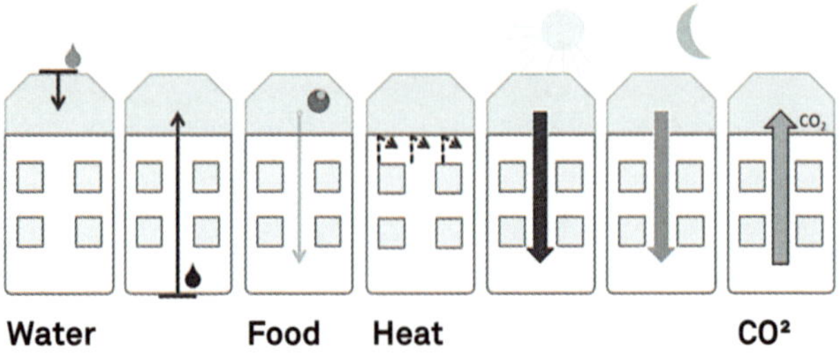

Roof

- Size
- Homogeneity
- Roof pitch
- Construction (load capacities)
- Microclimate / sun exposure
- Accessibility
- Infrastructure provision
- Spaces for amenities, storage, packaging

Building

- Zoning and building codes
- Other building uses
- Height
- Accessibility
- Infrastructure provision, logistics issues
- Need for renewal
- Integration in built environment

Neighborhood

- Urban fabric (densities, architecture, etc.)
- Socio-demographic character
- Potential interactions
- Social and transport infrastructure

City

- Urban fabric (densities, architecture, etc.)
- Policies
- Markets
- Urban and regional food system

SCULPTING MOUNTAINS

THOMAS CORBASSON, co-founder of CORBASSON-CHARTIER ARCHITECTS, argues against the division between building and nature. With his building for the Regional Chamber of Commerce and Industry, he demonstrates an outstanding example of a building that merges and combines the spheres of plant life and architecture. In his point of view, architects need new ways of designing—not against nature, but including and considering it in the design process.

FOOTBALL TRAINING CENTER
AMIENS, FRANCE, 2008

One of the first buildings we designed was a football training center. It was a challenge to redefine the limit between town and nature. The story we have to tell is a story about nature.

THOMAS CORBASSON: "The football training center creates a dialogue between the controlled, domesticated nature artificially represented by football pitches and the untamed greenery on the banks of the River Selle. The turf mantle is deformed and adapted to cover the building in order to create continuity with the existing landscape, while the building merges with the football field.

The big glass opening from one side to another allows a great connection of the interior with the riverside and the exterior vegetation."

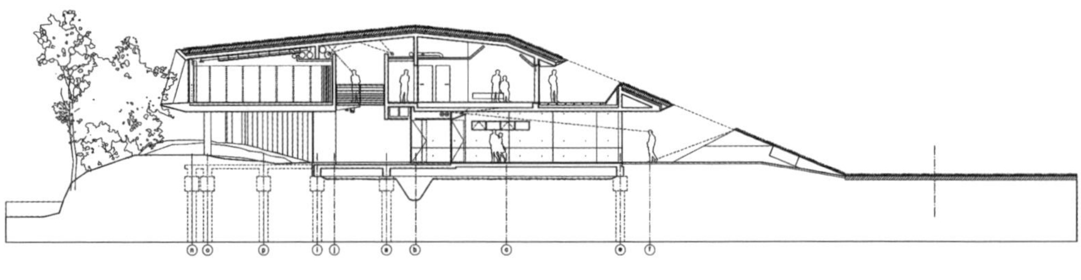

REGIONAL CHAMBER OF COMMERCE AND INDUSTRY
AMIENS, FRANCE, 2009

On the garden side, the building is the continuation of the existing landscape. The garden is folded to create the façade of the building, while the interior is orientated toward it with big openings that cut through the green façade. It is a fluid, continuous shape.

"Somehow, the Chamber for Commerce and Industry was slightly inspired by Greek architecture. I happen to have visited Greece at that time and I was intrigued by the philosophy of its architecture. Therefore, and after great contemplation, I believe that what defines this type of architecture the most is its relationship with the landscape.

It's not easy to work with landscaping architecture. We first began with a study model made with modelling clay, and then developed the idea by cutting the shapes we wanted into it.

When it came to actually building the fluent form, we only used prefabricated elements to adapt the green façade to the drawn shape, which is a double curved surface. The structural engineers had to calculate the exact angle of each premade piece of the 17-meter-long structure.

We chose the vegetation according to their characteristics, such as their colors or textures and their ability to adapt to the environment: for example, we wanted something very colored in the area that is the focus point of the view when you arrive.

When it comes to the interiors, a big hall which was designed to be like a cave makes the transition from the exterior to the interior."

"If you continue to build constructions against nature, there will be no nature. So we have to find a new way and a new word. For example, why not Hortitecture?" THOMAS CORBASSON

1

2

1 Acropolis, Athens
2 Gunkanjima Island

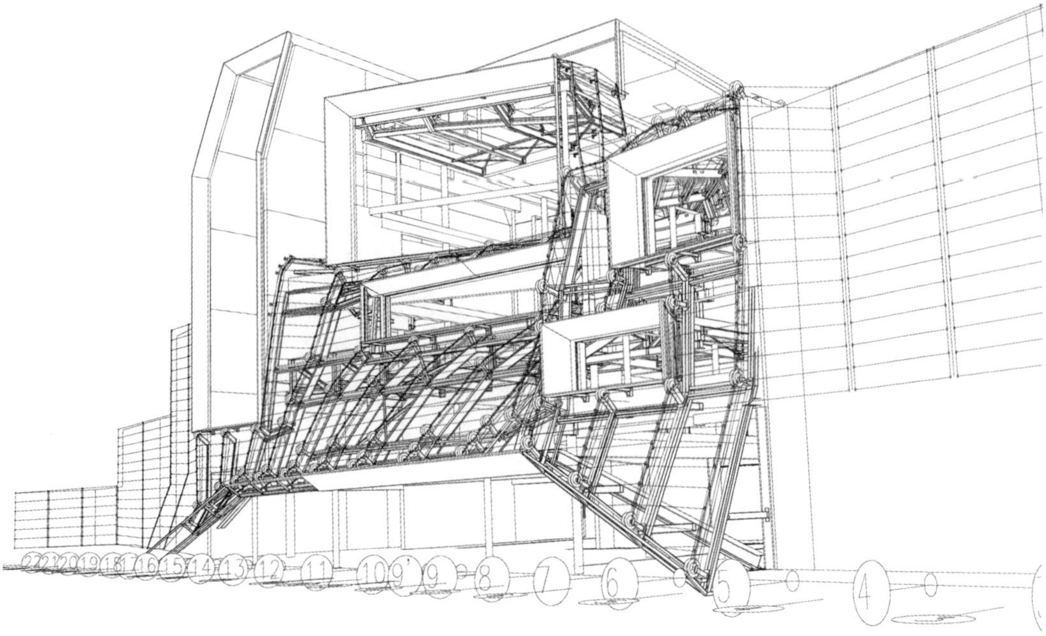
22 21 20 19 18 17 16 15 14 13 12 11 10 9' 9 8 7 6 5 4

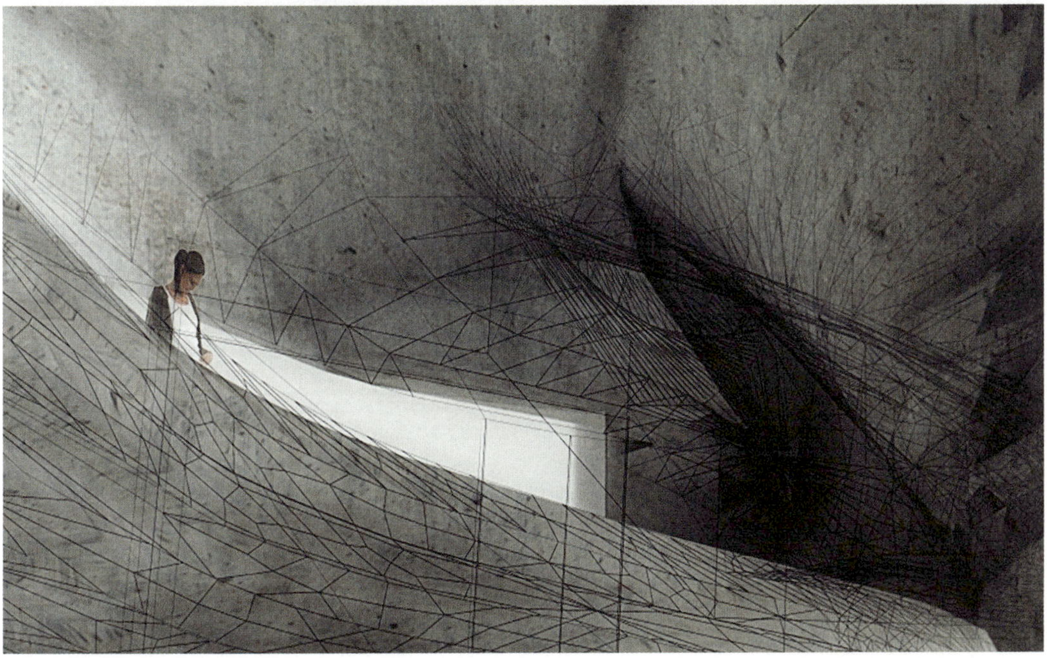

"It is about the idea of continuity. The building merges within the landscape and so it becomes an extension of the perspective.

The architect always has a complete understanding of the building and its relationship with its environment. The relationship with the landscape, however, remains different from the experience a landscaper might have: when I am doing Hortitecture, for example, I am not really a landscaper, because I am not drawing a landscape, I am drawing buildings with vegetation. Which requires a minimum knowledge about plants, of course, but it will not be as developed as the specialist's."

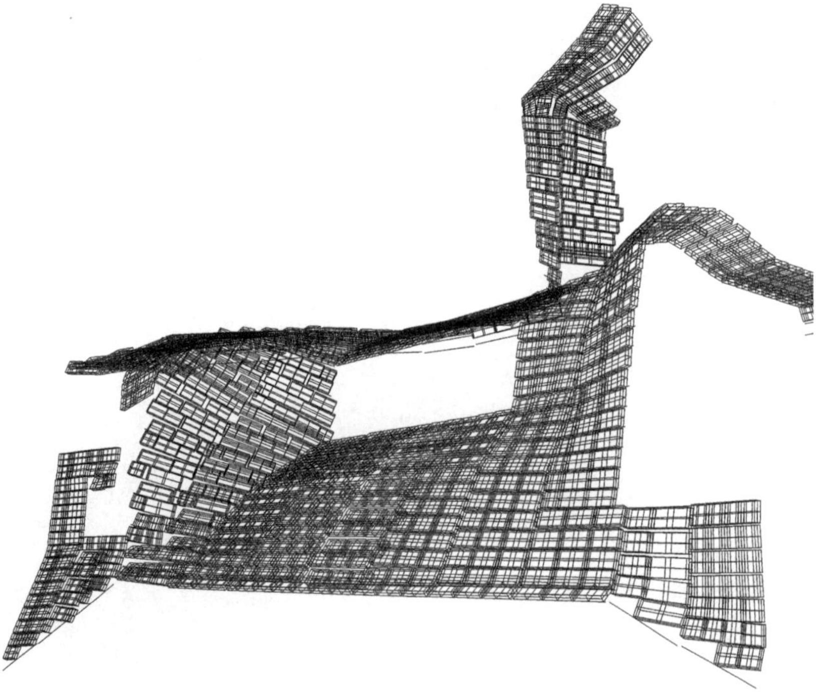

"I think if I want to say something, it is to stop opposing nature and buildings and to try to do better work with better building; including, in fact, vegetation, plants, and the way of working with building a city."

THOMAS CORBASSON

TEXTILE FARMING

Using the solar energy of urban vertical surfaces to grow food in the cities is the goal of NIKLAS WEISEL. He is the founder of BOXOM, a company developing new textiles based in vertical greening technologies. NIKLAS WEISEL also experiments with innovative façade-leasing concepts as an economic use of vertical surfaces in order to revolutionize the means of urban food production.

The vertical greening system is currently being developed by the companies BOXOM and B+M Textil. The system, Botanic Horizon, can be used indoors and outdoors. As a modular agricultural system, it activates the façades of urban buildings to produce food. Therefore, the system increases the living quality in cities and also contributes to their possibilities for self-supply In order to be more independent from conventional agricultural mass production.

NIKLAS WEISEL: "We are a developer of ropes, and we fill these ropes with seeds—and the seeds and the ropes are watered top-down with an irrigation system. The seeds then start to sprout and grow out of the ropes.

Our basic system is like a technology hub for all useful systems greening the façade. We also developed something called the strawberry curtain. We tried out what we can do with that, and we grew kohlrabi. On one cubic meter we grew about 100 kohlrabi. The one on the picture is 700 grams, exactly like the one from the supermarket. In another system we grew parsley.

I cannot walk through this world without thinking: 'Oh my god, such a waste of energy' because our buildings are collecting so much solar energy without using it. I want to use existing space. I came up with a little balance equation: 'Energy × Area = Food.'"

"Instead of fighting against the heat islands with air conditioning, we could use this energy to produce food and activate the vertical façades and their potential for agriculture—and at the same time cool the building by using the plants as shading and evaporation devices." NIKLAS WEISEL

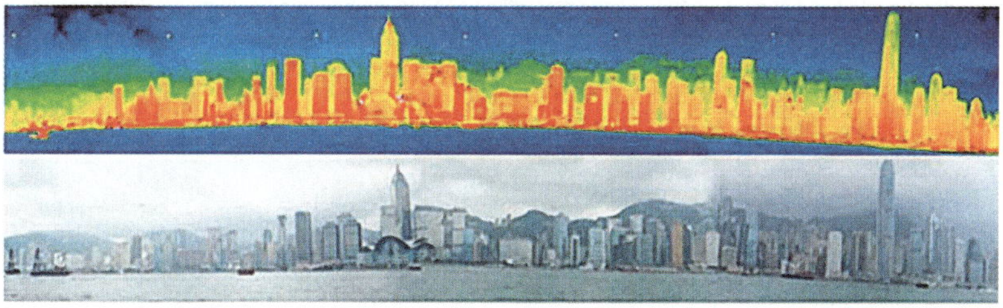

"The technology that we have has the advantage that it is affordable to everyone, and that it adapts automatically to the season: in springtime, the façade is very open, and in the summertime, it absorbs so much sunlight and energy—so you can grow and harvest a lot of things, and it regenerates in the meantime.

In the future, we will combine the technologies of both systems. You can use your façade to produce electricity with the solar panels in combination with plants.

We are thinking about a business model for tenants for façade farming. The question is 'when is it beneficial for the tenant and when is it beneficial for the owner?' You have to take those things into account. For example, how much can you harvest, how big is the benefit of the installation to the facility, and is there a combination that makes sense to the property owner—like, for example, cooling energy savings, which can cost quite a lot, or possibilities for storm water management? Without any automation technology today one person could maintain 2,800 square meters in eight hours per day."

"That's the idea. With this system you have a food-producing, decorative green façade that you can maybe even sell as a product and make some kind of business out of. And the maintenance of the green façade may be compensated by the harvest income." NIKLAS WEISEL

FARMING TEXTILES

DIANA SCHERER explores the dynamics of below ground plant parts and the relationship between man and his natural environment, as well as his desire to control nature. The starting point is the ambiguous tendency of man to cherish nature, but also to manipulate in a reckless way.

INTERVOVEN
AMSTERDAM,
2012–ONGOING

As an artist and photographer, Diana Scherer is captivated by the root system with its hidden underground processes. Her interest started with a rootbound pot plant. Fascinated by the structure of the roots, Diana Scherer started experimenting with different plants and vases to explore different types of rootbounds pot plant. From these discoveries, she started to develop rugs, exploring possibilities for directing the growth of the roots into patterns. Eventually, textiles resulted from these ongoing exercises in root system domestication, as a new kind of material.

"DIANA SCHERER: *Interwoven* is a project about plant roots. I discovered all the different kinds of structures, shapes, and colors of the shaped root systems.

I found a technique for weaving the roots. I have developed templates and I put them belowground in the soil, and after a while roots of my grass grow into the templates and follow the patterns I designed.

I generally show the three parts in an exhibtion; the photography, the fresh piece of art, and the dried root material.

I have different techniques to produce the templates. I design them digitally and then they are 3D-printed."

"I am still working on getting it stronger and have a whole investigation into different kinds of plants roots. The grain is great for artwork, but for real material—for example insulation, curtains, or carpets—it has to become much stronger.

One advantage of my material is absorbing carbon during the work process. I don't know that many artworks that can help the environment, but this one does.

I did different experiments with density, structure and I also tried to combine real fabrics with the roots to investigate the strength and appearance of the material.

I was looking for applications of the natural material and I started with a dress—a growing dress for an exhibition at V&A in London."

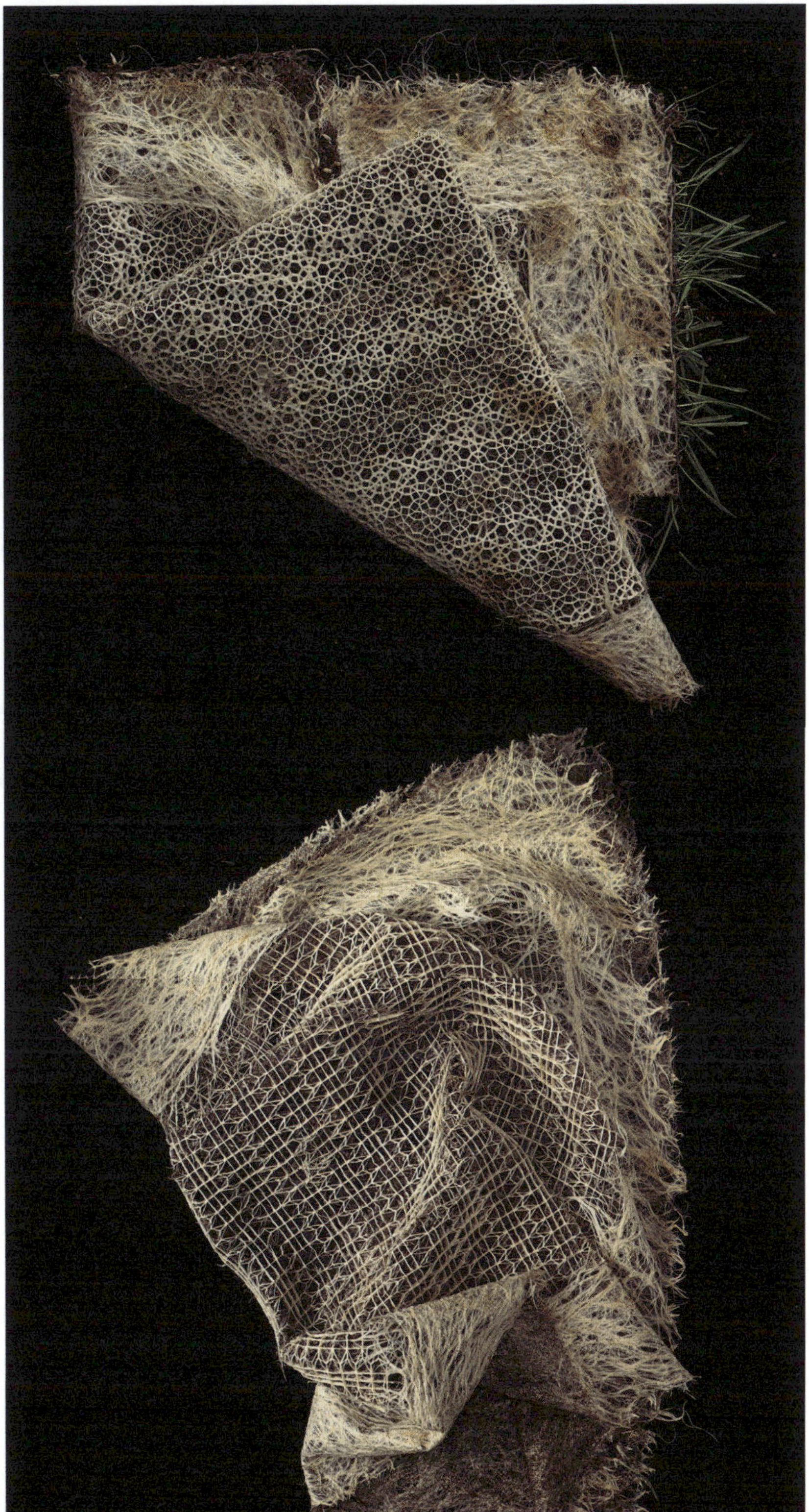

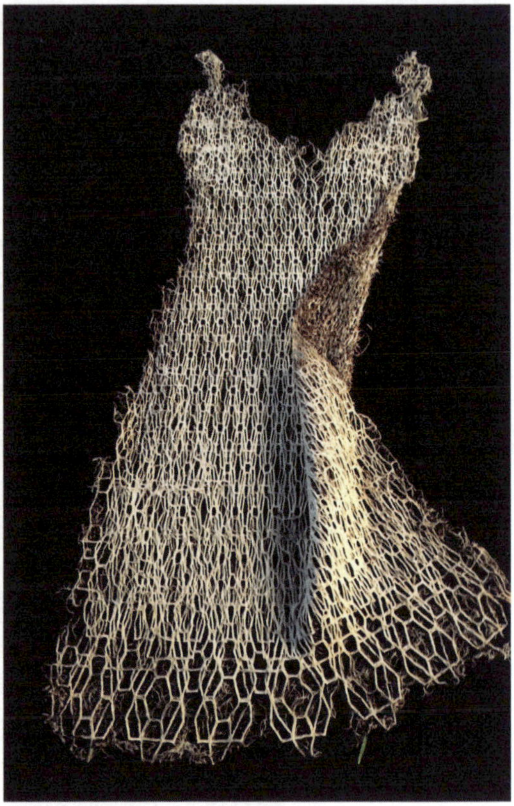

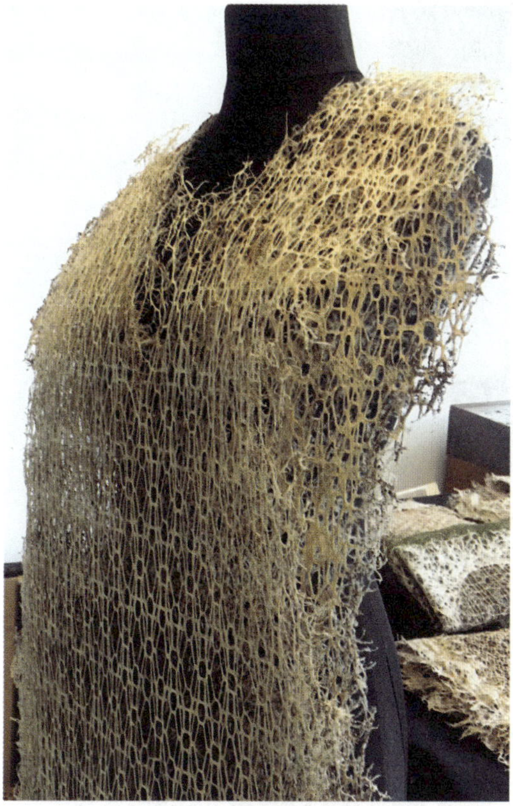
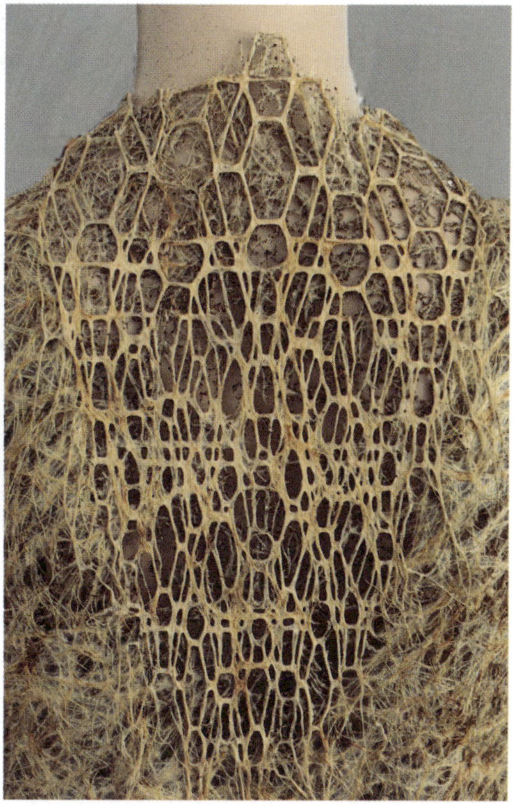

"This textile from plant roots is a natural material. The advantage, I think, is that because it weaves itself below the ground, you don't need an artificial weaving machine. Once I find the process of how to make it as strong as possible and find the right roots to make the weaving very strong, it could be suited for many things in architecture."

DIANA SCHERER

Fragile

GREEN TOWERS

With White Walls in Nicosia and One Central Park in Australia, ELISABETH KATHER at ATELIERS JEAN NOUVEL worked on two impressive green high-rises in order to combine plants and architecture. The projects always look for new ways of combining architecture and nature.

TOUR 25—WHITE WALLS
NICOSIA, CYPRUS, 2015

White Walls is an apartment and office tower in Nicosia in Cyprus designed by Ateliers Jean Nouvel. The south façade is a vertical landscape that covers 80% of the building's façade area with Cypriot climbing and spreading plants. The plants function as a natural sun-control shield in the summer but still admit a maxium of sunlight in winter. The floor plan is inspired by the Cypriot traditional architecture that organizes different rooms around one courtyard.

ELISABETH KATHER: "For Greek people, the combination of nature and architecture is no problem. But for Australian people it was unimaginable to put nature in the city; for them, those were two different things and not at all compatible.

I was going back into the office and telling Jean Nouvel that they cannot imagine architecture with nature together, and he couldn't believe it. Several months later he told me: 'You are right, there isn't a single plant on the balconies.' It was very hard to convince the Australians to combine nature with a building. The Australians have a dangerous natural habitat with spiders and snakes that they of course don't want to have in their flats."

"The classical way of architecture is to try to know everything that you are planning. The plants show you it is not possible. When an architect is honest, he knows that it is not possible to plan everything, because it is so complex. There is a new formation every day and we need to act on those things. And that's exactly what the plants are doing." ELISABETH KATHER

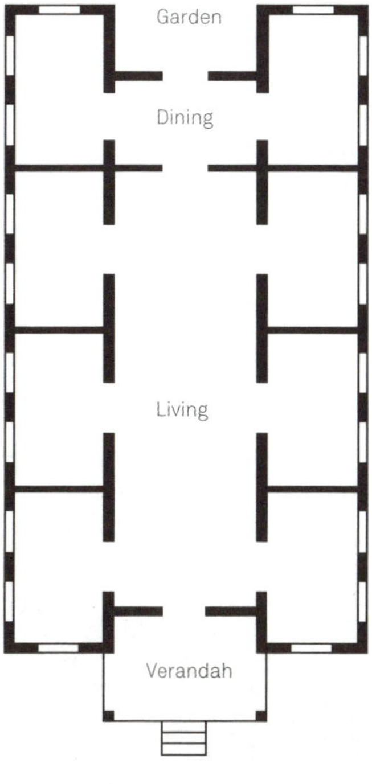
Garden
Dining
Living
Verandah

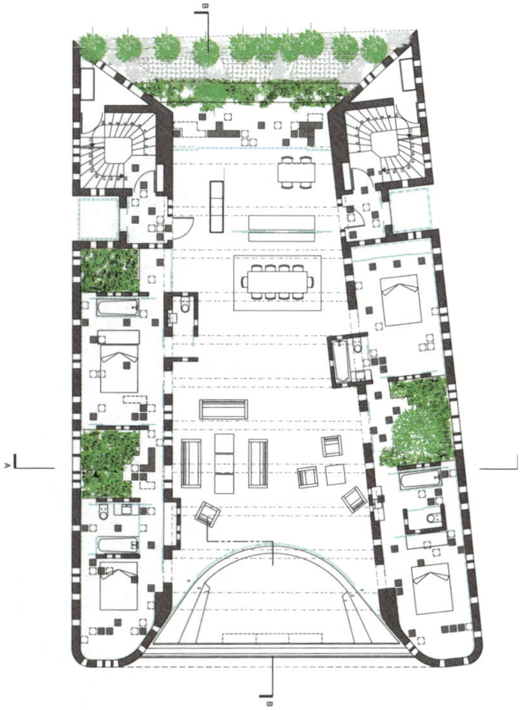

"What is interesting is that the building isn't finished at all because the plants are growing so well, and every time I am there I am very surprised by its ever-changing appearance and its changing over time.

My favorite garden is the smallest one. It was a nice experience in that, even with all the visualizations we did, the realization was a big surprise with regard to the sizes and also the light effects and framing of all the different surroundings."

"I think the plants give the architecture the possibility to change every time and to get better every year." ELISABETH KATHER

FRASERS BROADWAY
SYDNEY, AUSTRALIA, 2014

The two towers of Frasers Broadway were designed by Ateliers Jean Nouvel. The vertical landscape that covers 50% of the façade of the building was designed by the French botantist and artist Patrick Blanc. The vertical landscape is an extension of the urban park in order to create an exceptonal living environment.

"The idea was to realize vertical landscaped façades on the north and east side, and on the south and on the west side horizontal terraces falling like waterfalls to the public park side.

We imagined having a multitude of different species and we managed to work with Patrick Blanc on this project. He has a lot of experience with vertical green vegetation walls and he is a botanical researcher of Australians plants. He is someone who is always searching for new plants that can be integrated into vertical building structures.

The heliostat on the lower tower catches the sunlight and reflects it to the heliostat of the higher building to bring light into the atrium, to the park, and to every place that would be shaded otherwise."

"I think we should integrate more climate and energy aspects in the buildings in order to have an answer to the climate problem and to address important future problems."

ELISABETH KATHER

OUTLOOK

Architectural design is a form of research and creative exploration. What I connect with the term HORTITECTURE emerged from a personal interest, and is becoming a growing challenge in our architectural practice.
At GRÜNTUCH ERNST ARCHITECTS we work on proposals and built experiments trying to reconnect, repair, and rebalance the human being with nature in the built environment.
With the increasing digitalization and dematerialization of the world around us, close contact to plants in an urban environment is important—it gives us a full, sensual experience of life and time.
With the increasing density of cities, additional buildings should not only have a high architectural quality, but at the same time activate surfaces with living plants that could effectively enhance wellbeing and reduce our footprint on the built environment. Nature-based architectural strategies aim for more urban vitality.

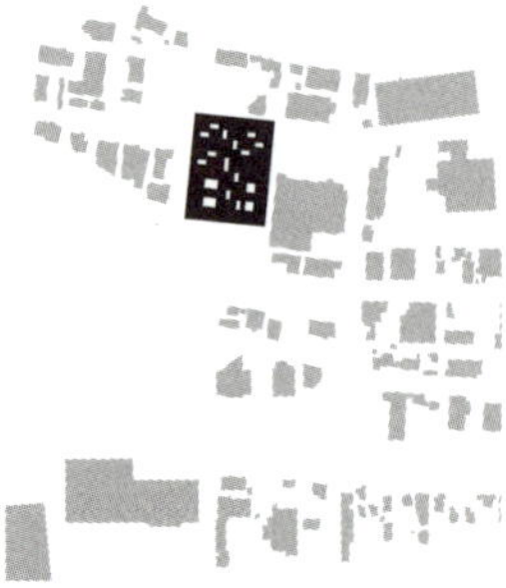

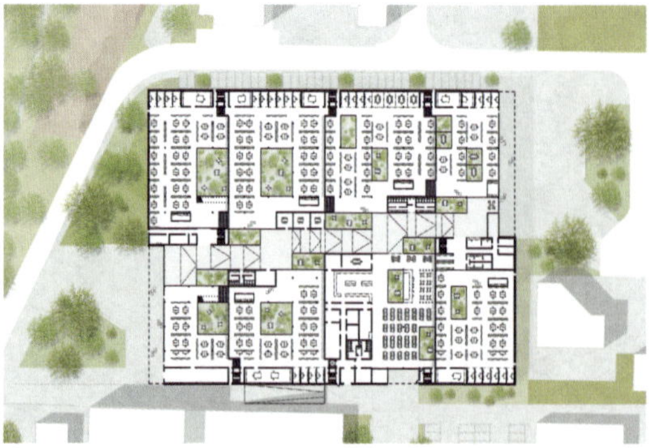

BALLUFF CAMPUS
NEUHAUSEN,
FIRST PRIZE 2017

The open-plan hall is perforated by "green islands" that provide informal working spaces shared with plants for inspiration, recreation, teamwork, and collaboration. The green islands structure the open-plan workplace, allow for natural respiration, and let the building breathe. We won the competition to design a green campus for Balluff, a leading provider of sensors, identification, and networking solutions for all areas of automation. In this unique nature-based working atmosphere, new ideas can emerge for sustainable future development.

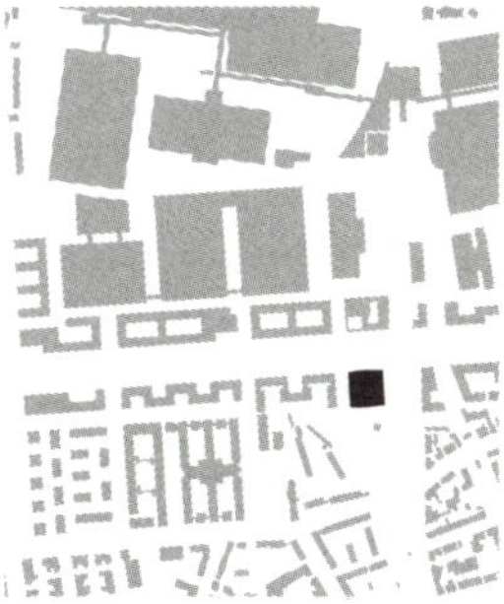

PORSCHE DESIGN TOWER
FRANKFURT,
FIRST PRIZE 2014

Rising from a glass atrium level is a tapered sculptural structure, with dark parapet bands that encompass the building and bring together its various typologies and usages, including apartments, townhouses, and parking. A generous green layer of plants along the parapets forms a conscious architectural element that adds a vital green layer to the purist façade and provides linear gardens for the residents.

AXEL SPRINGER CAMPUS
BERLIN,
SHORTLIST 2015

We were invited to submit to the competition design for the new Axel Springer Campus. The main idea of two interlocking spirals is based on the double-helix, and connects areas of conventional office space to green places of undedicated space. This allows for a stimulating stroll across all floors through the whole building. Conventional workspaces extend into exposed stages of inviting, green, and unbiased space.

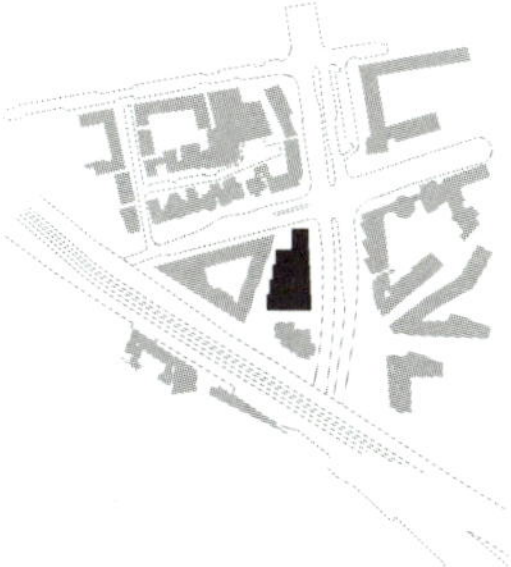

ÄRZTEKAMMER
HANNOVER,
FIRST PRIZE 2017

The new head office of the Chamber of Physicians in Hannover combines the functions of an efficient office building with a modern training centre. The building is composed of staggered levels with cascading green rooftop gardens. The green roof areas provide a direct connection to nature at the workplace and contribute to the microclimatic improvement in the urban space, as well as to an ecologically sustainable building operation. A healthy working environment and place of urban vitality!

MARTHASHOF
BERLIN, 2012
FIRST PRIZE 2006

On a former vacant lot in Berlin's Prenzlauer Berg district, the Marthashof residential development reacts to the diversity of urban lifestyles and communities with a wide range of apartment types and sizes, with both private and communal open spaces. For urban living environments we design buildings by interweaving grey and green spaces that connect the quarter to the surrounding city as a new urban module.

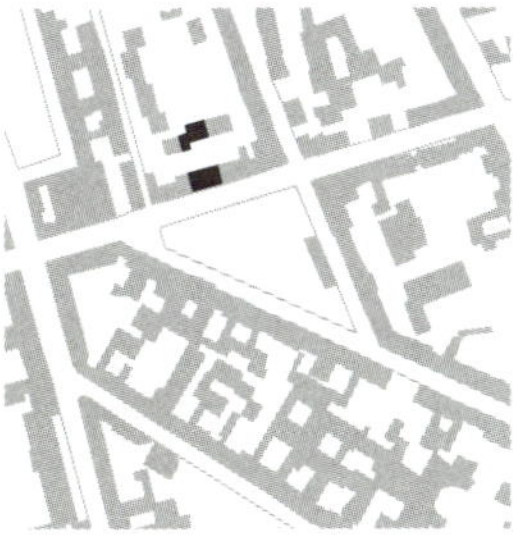

AUGUSTSTRASSE 51
BERLIN, 2009

An empty lot in Berlin's Spandauer Vorstadt neighborhood was the location for this co-housing building project, which combines the very diverse residential ideas with the needs of workplace, multi-generational living, and exhibition space. We share garden, courtyard, and rooftop spaces with urban gardening. In our office we enjoy the green interface around us with façades that have a supporting structure for plants to wrap around and frame the glass volume of the building.

academic research

As chair of IDAS, the Institute for Design and Architectural Strategies at the TU Braunschweig, my conceptual design work at the office is tightly connected to teaching and academic research. Some of our design studios at IDAS address biocentric questions, and thus build up awareness, critical reflection, and competence for sustainability and aspects of nature-based architecture that go beyond the status quo of fashionable greenwashing.

The building envelope has been optimized to control and maximize human comfort within the enclosed space, using less energy for heating, cooling, and ventilation. HORTITECTURE explores the performance of the building's exterior in order to also understand all kinds of multi-layered benefits while improving the microclimatic conditions of our cities. These methods no longer contrast city and nature, but explore new ways of them: designing buildings by interweaving grey and green spaces into ecosystems for holistic wellbeing.

HORTITECTURE will be a growing research subject which intends to cross-link core research disciplines of the Faculties of Architecture, Civil Engineering, and Environmental Sciences within the TU Braunschweig research focus *Future City/Stadt der Zukunft*.

We are building up interdisciplinary teaching cooperations and research teams. It is a great challenge to discover the potential of plant material for construction and the poetic power of compositions, and to link this viewpoint to the topics of food production and the provision of ecosystem services.

By studying the intersections between architectural, horticultural, and technological practices, as well as geoecological approaches and modelling, we envisage the transfer of knowledge for building design and beyond to a larger urban scope, creating better and more sustainable future cities.

Future City

APPENDIX

AUTHORS

Maria Auböck Landscape Architect studied architecture at the Technical University in Vienna. In 1987, she and János Kárász founded auböck+kárász. Their work has received numerous prizes and awards, including the Deutscher Städtebaupreis (2016) and the DAM Award (2018). She was a full professor at the Academy of Fine Arts in Munich from 1999 to 2018. She currently holds teaching positions in Vienna and Budapest.

Stefano Boeri Architect After a master's degree in Architecture from Milan Polytechnic in 1980 he received a PhD at the Istituto Universitario di Architettura di Venezia in 1989. In 1999 he founded Boeri Studio and later in 2008 Stefano Boeri Architetti. He was editor-in-chief of the architecture magazines *domus* and *Abitare*. Boeri is Professor of Urban Planning at Polytechnico Milano.

Gerhild Bornemann Ecologist works as a biologist at German Aerospace Center in Cologne. Her work includes the projects Eu:CROPIS and C.R.O.P.®, which deal with the evaluation of tomato growth in space and the reuse of wastewater in hydroponic greenhouses and life support systems.

Thomas Corbasson Architect studied at the Polytechnic University of Catalonia and the ENSA Paris-La Villette, where he earned his diploma in 1996. He was a project manager at Ateliers Jean Nouvel for ten years. Together with Karine Chartier he then founded Chartier-Corbasson Architects. He is currently the vice-president of the house of architecture of Île-de-France and teaches at the ESA (École Supérieure d'Architecture).

Almut Grüntuch-Ernst Architect studied architecture at the University of Stuttgart and the AA London, worked for Alsop & Lyall in London, and was a teacher at HdK Berlin. Together with **Armand Grüntuch** she founded Grüntuch Ernst Architects in 1991 in Berlin. In 2006 they were appointed German commissioners for the 10. International Architecture Biennale in Venice. Since 2011 she has been chair of the Institute of Design and Architectural Strategies at TU Braunschweig. She is a member of Akademie der Künste since 2016.

Richard Hassell Architect is the co-founding director of WOHA. He graduated from the University of Western Australia in 1989, and was awarded a Master of Architecture degree from RMIT University, Melbourne, in 2002. He has served as a board member of the Design Singapore Council, the Board of Architects, and the Building and Construction Authority of Singapore. He has lectured at many universities, and served as an adjunct professor at the University of Technology Sydney and the University of Western Australia.

Christoph Ingenhoven Architect studied architecture at the RWTH Aachen and at the Kunstakademie Düsseldorf. In 1985 he founded his office ingenhoven architects, which received international recognition with the design of the RWE Tower in Essen, one of the first ecological high-rise buildings in the world, in 1997. Numerous international awards followed. Ingenhoven is a founding member of the German Society for Sustainable Building.

Elisabeth Kather Architect graduated in architecture and engineering from the Technical University Darmstadt in Germany in 1993. She is a senior architect at Ateliers Jean Nouvel in Paris. Elisabeth Kather has been a project leader for many years and has gained a lot of experience mastering contextual and technical challenges. She has realized large projects in Germany, France, Russia, China, Australia, and Greece.

Klaus K. Loenhart Architect and Landscape Architect studied architecture at the Munich University of Applied Sciences, as well as Landscape Architecture and Design Studies in History and Theory at Harvard Graduate School of Design. In 2003, he founded terrain:, based in Munich and Graz. He became head of the Institute for Architecture and Landscape at Graz University of Technology in 2007, and has been part of the LANDLAB platform for interdisciplinary research.

Ferdinand Ludwig Architect studied at the University of Stuttgart and received a PhD on "Botanical basics of Baubotanik and their application to design practice." He is co-founder of the research group Baubotanik (Living Plant Constructions) at the University of Stuttgart, and is professor for Green Technologies in Landscape Architecture at the Technical University of Munich. At ludwig.schoenle, he works with Daniel Schönle on concepts in architecture and urbanism based on the ideas of Baubotanik.

Wilfrid Middleton Structural Engineer studied Civil Engineering (MEng) at the University of Bristol. He is a researcher at the Technical University of Munich, studying the living bridges of Meghalaya within the Professorship for Green Technologies in Landscape Architecture.

Nicola Moczek Psychologist studied psychology at the University in Frankfurt am Main. Together with Riklef Rambow, she founded PSY:PLAN, Institute for Environmental and Architectural Psychology. She is co-editor of the German scientific journal *Umweltpsychologie* (Environmental Psychology). Moczek works in the field of applied research and consulting on sustainable urban living and the perception and use of buildings.

Azzurra Muzzonigro Architect graduated from the Università degli Studi Roma Tre in 2009, and completed the MSc in Building and Urban Design in Development at the Bartlett School of Architecture in London 2011. In 2015, she obtained a PhD in Urban Studies at the Università degli Studi Roma Tre. Muzzonigro worked at Stefano Boeri Architetti as a research coordinator until 2017 and is adjunct professor of Architectural Design at Politecnico di Milano.

Vo Trong Nghia Architect Before returning to his home country Vietnam, where he established VTN Architects (Vo Trong Nghia Architects) in 2006, Vo Trong Nghia studied architecture at the University of Tokyo to earn his MA. His office is based in Ho Chi Minh City and Hanoi. Nghia has received international prizes and honours and was selected Architect of the Year in Vietnam in 2012. In 2011 he taught at the Nagoya Institute of Technology.

Fuensanta Nieto Architect has worked as an architect since graduating from the Universidad Politécnica de Madrid and the Graduate School of Architecture and Planning at Columbia University in New York in 1983. She is a founding partner of Nieto Sobejano Arquitectos and a professor at the Universidad Europea de Madrid. Fuensanta Nieto lectures on architecture and participates in juries and symposia at various institutions around the world. From 1986 to 1991 she was co-director of the architectural journal *ARQUITECTURA*, published by the Colegio Oficial de Arquitectos de Madrid.

Chris Precht Architect studied Architecture at the Technical Universities of Vienna and Innsbruck. In 2013 he founded Penda Architects together with Dayong Sun. The office is based in Beijing and Salzburg. Penda was ranked first on the Archipreneurs list for the World's Best Architectural Startups in 2016. Precht's work reflects his focus on the connection to a natural environment. His projects include the developement of different modular building systems.

Daniel Roehr Landscape Architect studied landscape architecture and horticulture in the UK. He is an associate professor at the University of British Columbia. He has run greenskinslab since 2007. His research focuses on the integration of living roofs as part of holistic systems for storm water management. He has practiced in Europe, North America, and Asia. He is currently developing an internationally usable Low Impact Development (LID) calculator. In 2013 he was a UBC Sustainability Research Fellow, and a Killam Teaching Prize winner in 2016.

Tomás Saraceno Artist and Architect Saraceno's oeuvre can be seen as an ongoing research, informed by the worlds of art, architecture, natural sciences, astrophysics, and engineering; his floating sculptures, community projects, and interactive installations propose and explore new, sustainable ways of inhabiting and sensing the environment. Saraceno lives and works in and beyond the planet Earth.

Diana Scherer Artist is a German-born artist and photographer based in Amsterdam. She studied fine arts and photography at Gerrit Rietveld Academy. She has published her work in numerous books and her work has been exhibited in galeries around the world, including Amsterdam, London, and Seoul. In 2016, her work was awarded the New Material Award.

Alina Schick Biologist studied biology with a focus on gravitational botany at the University of Bonn, and Marine Science at the University of Queensland in Brisbane. She holds a doctorate in agriculture from the University of Hohenheim. Her start-up company Visioverdis is developing innovative products that are a combination of technology and botany to solve problems typical for (mega) cities. Currently its most prominent product is the GraviPlant, a long-term caring system for plants which allows an alteration of environmental stimuli-sensing in small trees and other plants, allowing them to grow horizontally into space.

Marco Schmidt Environmental Planner studied Electrical Engineering and Environmental Planning at the Technical University Berlin. He is a research associate at Technische Universität Berlin, Chair of Building Technology and Design. Marco Schmidt coordinates and supervises the stormwater management, green façade, and irrigation system for the Institute of Physics Berlin-Adlershof and other sustainable architectural concepts.

Daniel Schönle Architect studied architecture and urban planning at the University of Stuttgart and graduated in 2002. Since 2008 he has been running his own planning office in Stuttgart. Daniel Schönle has taught at various universities. He is the co-founder of the office ludwig.schoenle—Baubotanik, Architecture, Urbanism. Since 2016 he has held a deputy professorship and headed the Urban and Regional Planning Unit at the Urban Development Institute of the University of Stuttgart.

Boris Schröder-Esselbach Geoecologist studies geoecology and philosophy at TU Braunschweig, where he has been a professor for landscape ecology and environmental systems analysis since 2013. As an expert in statistical and process-based modelling, he focuses on the effects of land use (change) on biodiversity and ecosystem services, and develops models for sustainable landscape management. Together with Vanessa Carlow, he is co-speaker of the TU Braunschweig research focus Future Cities.

Wong Mun Summ Architect is the joint founding director of WOHA. He graduated with honours from the National University of Singapore in 1989. He was a board member of the Urban Redevelopment Authority of Singapore and the Singapore Land Authority, and served as member of several design advisory panels for major developments in Singapore. He has mentored students under the National University of Singapore's Embedded Studio in Practice programme and, together with Richard Hassell, has served as Studio Masters for the University's MSc in Integrated Sustainable Design Masterclass since 2011.

Susanne Thomaier Researcher studied geography at the University of Bayreuth as well as Urban Affairs and Public Policy at the University of Delaware. In her research project Zero-Acreage Farming (ZFarming), Thomaier focuses on farming in and on urban buildings, including rooftop greenhouses, open rooftop farms, indoor farms, and productive façades. She is a research associate at the Technical University Berlin.

Jacob van Rijs Architect and Urban Planner is one of the founding principals of MVRDV, an interdisciplinary studio that works at the intersection of architecture and urbanism. With Winy Maas and Nathalie de Vries, the award-winning Dutch practice was set up over two decades ago and has established an international identity with a wide variety of building typologies and scales that are self-generated, innovative, experimental, and theoretical. Jacob's design ethos reflects a concern with user experience, micro homes, and a more humanistic approach to the built environment. This approach informs projects he leads on, including residential, social housing, and cultural and civic buildings.

Dieter Volkmann Biologist studied natural sciences in Würzburg, Tübingen, and Bonn. His dissertation addressed the perception of gravity, and his habilitation the dynamics of cells and membranes. He is emeritus professor at the University of Bonn with a research focus on communication in plants: neuronal aspects of plant life.

Marion Waller Philosopher and Urban Planner studied Urban Planning at Sciences Po Paris and Contemporary Philosophy at the École Normale Supérieure. She works as an advisor to the Deputy Mayor of Paris overseeing urban planning, architecture, and attractiveness, and has been the lead advisor on reinventer.paris competition. Her publication *Natural artefacts* deals with ecological restoration and new ethics for natural entities.

Stephan Weber Urban Climatologist studied physical geography at Ruhr-University Bochum, Germany. Currently, he is speaker of the expert committee Environmental Meteorology for the German Meteorological Society. He is also Professor of Climatology and Environmental Meteorology at the TU Braunschweig, and an expert in urban climatology, quantification of surface-atmosphere exchange using micrometeorological measurements, and urban aerosol research.

Niklas Weisel Environmental Engineer studied environmental- and bioengineering at the University of Bayreuth, at Dublin City University, and at Suwon Ajou University in Korea. He is founder and general manager of BOXOM GmbH and the brand Botanic Horizon—BoHo. Weisel is also company director and general manager at B+M Textil GmbH & Co. KG. He develops and realizes installing, irrigating, and supplying technology and systems for vertical gardens and fields of seed- and plant ropes.

Dan Wood Architect earned his masters degree in Architecture from Columbia University in 1992. He gained experience working for Rem Koolhaas/OMA in Rotterdam, later becoming the founder and president of AMO and OMA, New York. In 2003 he co-founded WORKac with Amale Andraos. He held the 2013–14 Louis Kahn Chair at the Yale School of Architecture and was an adjunct professor at Princeton University's School of Architecture.

Ken Yeang Architect and Ecologist was trained at the AA (Architectural Association) in London. Yeang has pioneered an ecology-based architecture since 1971, working on the theory and practice of ecological and sustainable design. He received a PhD from Cambridge University on the topic of ecological design and planning. His office, Hamzah & Yeang, has completed several eco high-rise buildings and earned many international awards. Yeang holds the Distinguished Plym Professor chair at the University of Illinois. The Guardian newspaper named him as "one of the 50 people who could save the planet."

Gerhard Zemp Gardener and Architect studied horticulture and later architecture at the ZHAW Zurich. In 2015, he founded aplantis, an architecture office specializing in building and interior greening. Gerhard Zemp is working on the interface between the artificial ground designed by the landscape architect and the building designed by the architect.

CREDITS AND REFERENCES

The editors have been careful to contact all copyright holders of the images used. If you claim ownership of the images presented here and have not been properly identified, please contact the Institute for Design and Architectural Strategies, TU Braunschweig. If not otherwise indicated, the copyright is with the respective authors or the Institute for Design and Architectural Strategies, TU Braunschweig.

Cover
U1, U4 Marco Garofalo 2012

Hortitecture
p. 6.1, 6.2 Public Domain p. 6.3 Ines Aubert p. 6.4 unbekannt p. 6.5 Future Systems, 1998 p. 6.6 Jason Benjamin Olav Havneraas p. 8.1 Tham& Videgard Arhitekter p. 8.2 Iona Marinescu p. 8.3 Nico Saieh p. 8.4 SITE, James Wines p. 8.5 Life Magazine, J. Walker p. 8.6 Boeri Studio p. 10.1 Tezuka Architects, Kida Katsuhisa\FOTOTECA p. 10.2 Kengo Kuma p. 10.3 Nieto Sobejano Arquitectos p. 10.4 Super-Limão Studio + Campanas Brothers p. 10.5 Timothy Brown p. 10.6 David von Becker p. 12.1 Visiondivision, Anders Berensson & Ulf Mejergren p. 12.2 XuTianTian Architects p. 12.3 Brooklyn Grange Rooftop Farm p. 12.4 WORKac p. 12.5 Thermo-System Krötz p. 12.6 Valcenteu p. 12.7 Omega Garden

Vertical Forest
p. 20 Marco Garofalo 2012 p. 22 Boeri Studio p. 23, 25.6, 27, 28 Stefano Boeri Architetti p. 25.1 Hundertwasser Archiv 2018/Aldo Cantarella p. 25.2 Public Domain p. 25.3 Superstudio p. 25.4 Andrea Branzi p. 25.5 Joseph Beuys VG Bild+Kunst p. 26, 32 Paolo Rosselli 2015 p. 29 blog.urbanfile.org p. 30, 33 Laura Cionci

Poetic Combination
p. 34, 36, 37.3, 38, 39.3 Roland Halbe p. 37.1, 37.2, 39.1, 39.2, 40, 40.1, 40.2 Nieto Sobejano Arquitectos

Green Power
p. 42, 47.1 MVRDV/Rob't Hart p. 44.1 The Why Factory p. 44.2 Luxigon p. 45.1, 45.2, 46, 47.2, 49, 50. 51.1, 51.2 MVRDV p. 48.1, 48.2, 48.3 José Carlos Melo Dias

Biosphere 3
p. 52, 55.3, 56, 57 Studio Tomás Saraceno p. 55.1 Public Domain p. 55.2 Hbarrison

Urban Biodiversity & Ecosystem Services
p. 58 Florian Möllers p. 60.1, 60.2 Jannik Heusinger p. 61.1 Nicole Pfoser 2014 p. 61.2 Elmqvist T et al. (Eds.). 2013. *Urbanization, Biodiversity and Ecosystem Services.* p. 62 Grunwald, L., Heusinger, J., & Weber, S. (2014). *Potentialanalyse zur Klimawirksamkeit von Gründächern in der Stadt Braunschweig als Instrument einer klimaschutzgerechten Stadt- und Bauleitplanung. Erhebung von Potentialflächen für Gründächer in Braunschweig.* 28 S. p. 63 Grunwald, L., Heusinger, J., & Weber, S. (2017). *A GIS-based mapping methodology of urban green roof ecosystem services applied to a Central European city. Urban Forestry & Urban Greening,* 22, 54–63.

Growth as a Concept
p. 64, 67.3 Cira Mora p. 67.1 http://www.landschaftsmuseum.de/Bilder/Album_33-Linde_Peesten-2.jpg p. 67.2 Anwesha22 p. 67.4, 67.5, 69.1 F.Ludwig p. 69.2 Boris Miklautsch, Uni Stuttgart p. 69.3, 69.4, 71.1, 71.2 ludwig.schönle

Houses for Trees
p. 72, 77.2, 78, 83.1, 83.2, 83.3 Hiroyuki Oki p. 75.1, 75.2, 75.3, 76, 77.2 Vo Trong Nghia Architects p. 81.1 Gremsy p. 81.2 Quang Tran

Nature City
p. 84 Iwan Baan p. 87 Elisabeth Felicella p. 89.1 WORKac (2016). *49 Cities* p. 89.2 Public Domain p. 91.1, 91.2 WORKac

Architectural Psychology
p. 92 Nicola Moczek p. 95 Mike Peel (www.mikepeel.net)

Biointegration
p. 96, 100.1, 100.2, 101., 103.1, 103.2, 103.3 TR Hamzah & Yeang Sdn. Bhd. p. 99, 102 IDAS p. 98 Yeang, K. (2009). *Eco Master Planning*

The Gravity of Plants
p. 106 Gustavo Alàbiso, Visioverdis GmbH p. 108 Visioverdis GmbH p. 109.1 Leif Piechowski p. 109.2 Public Domain p. 109.3 www.spacebio.uni-bonn.de

Urban Water Management
p. 110 greenskinslab 2009 p. 112.1 Daniel Roehr p. 112.2, 113.2 Roehr, D. & Fassman-Beck, E. (2015). *Living Roofs in Integrated Urban Water Systems* p. 113 Ryan L. C. Quan

Close Cycle Food Production
p. 114 Public Domain p. 116, 117.3, 119.3 DLR Institut für Luft- und Raumfahrtmedizin p. 117.1 Public Domain p. 117.2 Felix Riess p. 117.4, 119.1, 119.2 DLR (CC-BY 3.0) p. 119.4 Adriam Smith + Gordon Gill Architecture

Green River Milano
p. 120, 123.1, 123.2, 123.3 Stefano Boeri Architetti

Reinventing Paris
p. 124, 128.1, 128.2, 129.1, 129.2 Sou Fujimoto Architects + Manal Rachdi Oxo Architectes + Compagnie de Phalsbourg + Ogic + Morph p. 127.1 Public Domain p. 127.2, 127.3 Pavillon de l'Arsenal p. 130.1 City of Paris p. 130.2 Lina Ghotmeh Architecture p. 130.3, 130.4 XTU Architects p. 131.1 Mairie de Paris p. 131.2 Reindeer Renderings for David Chipperfield Architects

Living Climate Machine
p. 132 Simon Oberhofer p. 134 Institut für Architektur und Landschaft TU Graz p. 135.1, 135.3 Marc Lins p. 135.2 Daniele Madia p. 136, 137.1, 137.2, 137.3, 138, 139 team.breathe.austria

Supergreen
p. 140, 142, 144.1, 144.2, 144.3, 144.4, 144,5, 144.6, 144.7, 144.8, 145, 148, 149.1, 151.1, 151.2, 151.3, 151.4 ingenhoven architects p. 143, 146, 147 HGEsch p. 149.2 Can Stock Photo/horakgrafik p. 149.3 Pixabay, deidi p. 149.4 Pixabay, Hans

Garden City Mega City
p. 152 Flickr, HeyltsWilliam (https://www.flickr.com/people/heyitschili/) p. 155.1, 157.2, 157.4, 158, 159, 160.1, 161.1, 161.2, 162.1, 163.2 Patrick Bingham-Hall (2016). *Garden City Mega City: Rethinking Cities for the Age of Global Warming* p. 155.2 Public Domain p. 155.3, 157.1, 157.3, 160.2, 162.2, 162.3 WOHA p. 163.1 Albert Lim KS

Indoor Landscapes
p. 166, 171.1, 172, 173 aplantis p. 169.1, 169.2 Philipp Schäfer Architekten, 1930 p. 169.3 Arne Jacobson, Liselotte Orgel-Köhne, 1958 p. 169.4, 169.5 Stiftung Haus Schminke, Ralf Ganter p. 169.6 Haefeli, Moser, Steier p. 17.2, 171.3 Foster + Partners p. 175.1, 175.2, 175.3 VOGT

Growing Bridges
p. 176, 179.1, 179.2, 181, 183.1, 183.2, 183.3 Wilfrid Middleton

Cooling Urban Heat
p. 184, 190 Marco Schmidt p. 187.1, 187.5, 188.1, 188.2, 188.3, 193.1, 193.2 Marco Schmidt, Baluška, Mancuso, Volkmann Communication in Plants Neuronal Aspects of Plant Life, Springer 2006 p. 187.2, 187.3, 187.4 Marco Schmidt, Data: physicalgeography.net, Graphic: IDAS p. 189.1, 189.2, 191 Simon Menges

Stacking Green
p. 194, 197.2, 197.3, 198, 199.1, 199.2, 200, 201.1, 201.2, 201.3, 201.4, 201.5, 202, 203, 204.1, 204.2, 205.1, 205.2 PENDA Studio p. 196 Pixabay, 3dman_eu p. 197 Pixabay, roheryn319

Building Landscapes
p. 206, 211.1, 211.2, 211.3 Maria Auböck p. 209.1 *Spanish and Portuguese gardens/Nichols;* boston: Houghon Mifflin Co., 1924 p. 209.2 Fischer von Erlach, Stich p. 209.3 alamy p. 209.4 Vanessa Mendes Argenta p. 209.5 Groume p. 212.1 Ivana Kucirkova p. 212.2 Schreieck Architects, Auböck-Kárász Landscape Architects p. 213.1, 213.2 Pfau p. 214 David Riek, bauchplan p. 215.1 Michael Heinrich p. 251.2 bauchplan

Communication in Plants
p. 216 Carl Davies, CSIRO p. 219.1 Lichtenegger et al. Stapfia 49 (1997). *Wurzeln: Bewurzelung von Pflanzen in verschiedenen Lebensräumen* p. 219.2 Jagadish Chandra Bose, Life movements of plants 1918/1926 p. 220 Graphic: IDAS p. 221 Bonfante, P. & Genre, A. Mechanisms underlying beneficial plant–fungus interactions in mycorrhizal symbiosis. Nat. Commun. 1:48, fig. 3, doi: 10.1038/ncomms1046 (2010).

Zero Acreage Farming
p.222 Susanne Thomaier p. 225.1 Jenny Sherouse Photography p. 225.2 Valcenteu p.225.3 Thomaier el al. (2014) *Vertical Farming Association* (https://vertical-farming.net) p. 226 inter 3 Institut für Ressourcenmanagement GmbH p. 227.1, 227.2 Susanne Thomaier

Sculpting Mountains
p. 228, 231.1, 231.2, 234, 239 Yves Marchand & Romain Meffre p. 230, 236, 237.2, 238 Chartier-Corbasson architectes p. 233.1 Gfmichaud p. 233.2 Jordy Meow p. 237.1 Ludovic KITEL

Textile Farming
p. 240, 242.1, 242.2, 243.1, 243.2, 245, 247 BOXOM p. 243.3 Professor Yuguo Li, Built Environment Group p. 246.1, 246.2, 246.3 IDAS

Farming Textiles
p. 248, 250, 251.1, 251.2, 251.3, 252.1, 252.2, 253.1, 253.2, 254.1, 254.2 255.1, 255.2 Diana Scherer

Green Towers
p. 256, 258, 259.1, 260, 261.1, 261.2 Yiorgis Yerolymbos p. 259.2 Ateliers Jean Nouvel p. 259.3 Design architect: Ateliers Jean Nouvel; collaborating architects: Takis Sophocleous Architects p. 261.3 Design architect: Ateliers Jean Nouvel. Local collaborating architect: PTW Architects p. 262, 263 Roland Halbe

Outlook
p. 266–273 Grüntuch-Ernst Architekten p. 274 IDAS, Jan Bitter

Impressions
p. 282–285 IDAS
p. 288 Frei Otto: *Zur Zukunft* 1999. published in *Geplante Poesie*, Editor Stadt Leonberg, 2001

TECTURE
RTITECTURE
03

TEAM AND SPONSORS

International symposia at the Technische Universität Braunschweig on 10.12.2014, 15.11.2016 and 15.11.2017

Research Team
Felix Henri Rebers, Kristien Ring,
André Schmidt, Ana Zatezalo-Schenk

Support Team
Silke Stöckel, Alexander Butz, Anna Berger, Maike Bodenbender,
Niklas Graage, Jannis Petereit, Vincent Szur, Julia Windeler,
Michael Batelka, Marisa Bergmann, Laura Brüggemann,
Jan Leonard Goldenbaum, Clemens Wiese, Benedikt Engelke
Fred Plassmann (OFFscreen Filmproduction)

We thank the sponsors whose support made these events possible:

U.S. Consulate General Hamburg
Istituto Italiano di Cultura Berlino – Italienisches Kulturinstitut Berlin
GOETHE INSTITUT

Niedersächsisches Ministerium für Soziales, Gesundheit und Gleichstellung
Ecki Wohlgehagen-Stiftung
LAVESSTIFTUNG

Holcim
KATHARINA VON EHREN INTERNATIONAL TREE BROKER GMBH
Braunschweigische Landessparkasse – Ein Unternehmen der NORD/LB

HELIX PFLANZENSYSTEME
ÖFFENTLICHE VERSICHERUNG BRAUNSCHWEIG
KWS

IMPRINT

Editor
Prof. Almut Grüntuch-Ernst
Institute for Design
and Architectural Strategies

TU Braunschweig
Pockelsstraße 3, 15. OG
D-38106 Braunschweig

Telefon +49 (0)531 391-94400
E-Mail idas@tu-bs.de
Internet idas.tu-bs.de

Head of Publication
Felix Henri Rebers

Publication Team
Florian Thein, Maike Bodenbender,
with Anna Kostreva, Tom Kalkhoven

Design and setting
Moniteurs, Berlin,
Sibylle Schlaich, Anna Gaißmaier

Cover: Collage IDAS, Marco Garofalo
Proofreading: Jessica Glanz
Lithography: Bild1Druck, Berlin
Printed in the European Union

Bibliographic information published by the Deutsche Nationalbibliothek
The Deutsche Nationalbibliothek lists this publication in the Deutsche Nationalbibliografie; detailed bibliographic data are available on the Internet at http://dnb.d-nb.de

jovis Verlag GmbH
Kurfürstenstraße 15/16, 10785 Berlin

www.jovis.de

jovis books are available worldwide in select bookstores. Please contact your nearest bookseller or visit www.jovis.de for information concerning your local distribution.

ISBN 978-3-86859-547-5

"A truly ecological architecture, one that is both energy- and material-saving and promotes human integration with nature as a whole, can be regarded as one of the great tasks of the future."

FREI OTTO 1999